PARADOX

FREEDOM EQUALITY
TUG OF WAR

Glen Smith

FREEDOM of the Young Colt

In late Spring
The mighty stallion, leader of the mustang herd, jumped the enclosure and achieved freedom. The young colt followed but could not jump high enough to escape.

One Spring morning his mother gave birth. He loved the taste of his mother's milk and wobbled freely in the new green grass.

Summer
The colt gained strength and felt his power as he saw the mighty mustangs which ruled his wild herd.

In early Spring mares began to give birth to foals. As grass sprouted he yearned for the open plains. Young stallions were broken for saddles and given their liberty in the big pasture.

Life of the Herd

In early Autumn the soft grass dried up and his mother was hungry. The coyotes roamed the night searching for young animals. Fear struck the young colt.

In late Winter mares' withers showed hope for new births. Some of the mighty stallions were rounded up and locked away in trailers.

Late Autumn
With their ropes the ranchers came quickly. The colt's mighty herd was restricted in round pens and then moved into a large fenced enclosure and fed. Electric lights kept the coyotes at distance. Fear disappeared.

Throughout the Winter wind blew snow, like sharp sand, into the colt's eyes. The colt was at peace and secure because he knew the cowboys had kept him safe.

Tug of War Definitions

Definitions are approximate and related to context:

ONE: One individual human organism.

EVERY: Set of all individual human organisms considered as a defined group, all living humans, or all humans who have lived, are living, or shall live (humanity as a total concept).

EVERYONE: One person as an undifferentiated singularity representing all humanity, an abstract blend combining opposite concepts (**ONE** and **EVERY**). It is a utilitarian and normative fantasy with no concrete reality.

EACH PERSON: Differentiated individual who has genetic and environmental qualities which permit him to be perceived as unique by other singular humans (a real, concrete human being).

GOVERNMENT: Organized group of individuals with the expressed purpose of mediating the relationship of **FREEDOM** to **EQUALITY** within a geographic area that includes a culture or set of cultures.

FREEDOM: Each person decides personal action and what his response to other individuals shall be. Therefore, cause and effect is a process of natural law and each person's understanding. **FREEDOM,** as a part of **NATURAL LAW,** is delegated by nature and God (or **FIRST CAUSE**). Just as other animals, man's choice of action begins at birth.

LIBERTY: **FREEDOM** is delegated by **NATURAL LAW.** In contrast **LIBERTY** is a condition of returned **FREEDOM/s** which has been taken away by the state and its **POWER.** For example, a wild and free animal is caged. Its captor then decides to liberate the animal and then releases it. It is given **LIBERTY**.

EQUALITY of OPPORTUNITY: Set of government's legal processes is standardized for **EACH PERSON** and conforms to the abstract fantasy of **EVERYONE**.

EQUALITY of EFFECT: Set of **EFFECTS** from personal **BEHAVIOR** ends in results that are undifferentiated and fit a normative concept of **EVERYONE** rather than based on an individual's actions. Unlike other animals, man's choice of action may consider the disparity in conditions of his birth.

TOTAL EQUALITY: Combination of **EVERYONE** fantasy with **EQUALITY** of

OPPORTUNITY and **EFFECT,** creating **STASIS** within a culture, set of cultures, or geographic area.

CHAOS: States of **FREEDOM** or **EQUALITY** without a mediating relationship between them.

ELECTION; Periodic process to insure a culture or nation has a mix of public and private organizations to insure a functional and harmonic political system posessing a mix of **FREEDOM**, **INVENTION**, **ENERGY** and **PRODUCTS** which is widely enough distributed within the society (**EQUALITY**) to prevent chaos or war.

JUSTICE: Highest, most effective combination and/or relationship regarding the contrasting values of **FREEDOM** and **EQUALITY** within a given duration of TIME and SPACE.

3

Freedom

Equality

ONE + EVERY = EVERYONE

Man's will to survive, to thrive, and to exercise his intellectual and physical power through freewill is his basic instinct. As a creature of nature he is both predator and prey; thus, he must constantly observe and evaluate his surroundings. Because other men are the most dangerous natural predators to each man's existence, humanity has devised and then propagated a code that promotes each person's survival within the family of other men. For both the religious and the atheist this concept, or code of conduct, is simply to confine his actions against other men to the actions he would have them do to him. Thus, in addition to his concept of himself, which is the **ONE**, designated "**I**", the concept of all other men, which is "**EVERY**", is created. Therefore, there is the internal self, **I** or **ONE**, which strives to survive, who constantly evaluates his relationship to all other men, **EVERY**, in order to not become prey. This dual nature creates the concept of **EVERYONE**. It promotes a continuous internal and external exchange between **ONE** and **EVERY**. This dual struggle, or **TUG OF WAR**, is both the eternal and the temporal nature of humanity. In this struggle both **FEAR** and **LOVE** are created.

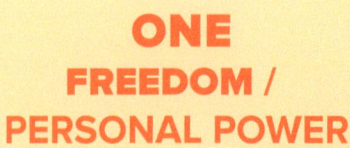

ONE
FREEDOM /
PERSONAL POWER

Social arteries for distribution of goods and services across entire culture

Positive effect: collective welfare
Negative effect: depletes cultural energy

EVERYONE
PUMP

POLITICAL
CIRCULATORY
SYSTEM

Social arteries feedback
Negative effect: inhibits distribution
Positive effect: reaffirms personal energy and creativity

EVERY
EQUALITY

Pathologies for Political Circulation include:

Inadequate production of cultural energy

Inadequate diffusion of political rights, goods and services (nutrients and energy) throughout body of culture

Erratic or excessive circulation pressures, or gaps, in cultural distributions

Disassociation of the neurological command operation of the circulation system with feedback sensory from the culture

External or internal stress which has negative impact on the needs of the culture

Setting the Stage
What is a game?

A formal construction with aesthetic form, rules of constraint, and statistical criteria which permit participants, physically and/or mentally, to engage in direct opposition, or polarity, and reach an unpredictable outcome. This outcome is intended to create an undisputed winner. The game's formal structure then permits the less fit, or loser, to survive.

What is the Origin of the Game?

The formal structure of the game is seen in nature. Male-female dominance and courtship and the evolution of pack leaders have involved rituals and formal conflicts which limit the injury in herd and pack members during dominance conflicts. A simple example is during the conflict for the alpha leadership of a wolf pack. The losing animal turns, belly up, and allows the alpha animal to place his jaws around the loser's neck.

What is the primary social character of all team games?

All team games must function with participating groups internally connected with political and social conditions that evoke polarity against the opposing team. The game's restraining structure and process achieve its outcome without absolute expression of force. In effect the game is the opposite of Carl von Clausewitz's concept in *On War* that war is an expression of politics without restraint. The team game is an expression of war with constraints and variables which permit civilized conflict resolution which can create clarity and aesthetic satisfaction for the participants and for spectators

What does government do?

One

U.S.

Every

Globe
(us & them)

Government HELPS organize and timely defines the relationship of ONE person to EVERY. EVERY is composed of "I/US" and "them". Thus government provides the voluntary and involuntary nervous system for the political circulatory system.

What is an example of a primal team game?

Tug of War was used in ancient China as a training element for the military. It exhibits the simplest formal construction to show the connection between restrained conflict (team games) and unrestrained conflict (war). This game is the prototype for the structure of the two party political system developed in the United States. The timing of the election system for President has its roots as far back as Greek history, in Olympiad, a unit of time measuring four years. The unit marked four years between Olympic Games.

What are the limits on the Tug of War Model?

Clausewitz and Marx concepts are 19th century models. Both contain characteristics of thought common to Darwin. Polarity and opposition are vital to Clausewitz in *On War*, Marx in his dialectic, and Darwin in the evolution of male and female animals. Resolution of this polarity is an end product for each of these models. These are the result of resolution of hostilities in war, historical synthesis in dialectics, and genetic synthesis during reproduction by male and female animals. This conceptual vector is mirrored in the development of two party systems within the United States; thus the **Tug of War** image. The polar concepts in Clausewitz, Marx, and Darwin are useful to organize thoughts. They cannot be applied on any universal basis. They do promote an understanding of the gaming system used to choose the chief executive of the United States and the participants: the Democratic Party and Republican Party. Marx fails to see that synthesis is organic and will die. The process then repeats in a continuous circular system that can have multiple natural pauses. The democratic pattern is circular and does not have a predicted historical end.

FREEDOM Utopian Natural Condition:
natural flux among creatures of unequal character to achieve dynamic balance (contrary to equality)

Divergent Variables

Personal freedom:
the natural right of each animal (person) to preserve himself and extend his power

Ascent of tribal "war lords" to create order

Deconstruction of the state:
power taken by individuals from the social collective

Personal liberty:
power given by the social collective to the individual for his self preservation

Freedom and Equality Historical Process Loop

Undifferentiated Variables

Construction of the State and regulation of individuals:
power taken by the social collective from the individual to promote peace

EQUALITY
Utopian Equality:
social collective distribution of equal power to individuals in order to preserve peace (contrary to freedom)

Potential "dictatorship of the proletariat"

9

The Stage: The Presidential Election

The Presidential Election in the United States is a team game played on a scheduled basis which allows for the civilized and restrained transfer of executive political power. Within the last 150 years this game has been played between two political teams, or parties, in a modern form of **Tug of War**. As in all games, standardized rules and patterns must be adhered to in order to keep politics restrained, create clarity, and provide aesthetic satisfaction for the participants, winners or losers. The uncivilized alternative to this functional game is a part of our history between 1861 and 1865.

The Presidential Election is an **EVERY/ONE** TUG OF WAR.

There are two areas of observation: 1. Structure and process of gaming, the system, timing, and rules of gaming, and 2. Construction and composition of the teams, or parties, in polarity for The Big-Green/Red Tug of War. Both the game and its parties can be observed through factors which predispose the character and stage the beginning of the election process. As the process evolves other enabling factors develop. Later factors reinforce and support the game's result after its completion.

What is the goal and process of election?

The **EVERY/ONE** **Tug of War** is represented in political context by the Democratic and Republican Parties. It is characterized in a duel to overcome with electoral and/or popular votes the opposing party to elect the President of the United States. Strategy demands an overall plan to acquire these votes at the date of election in as overwhelming quantity to the opposing party as possible. The process for each party consists of an exchange of reciprocal action, offensive and defensive. Tactics are how these specific actions are orchestrated. The environment includes electronic, print, and social media, geographic and legal factors, religious and ethical factors, national and international events, and the character of groups targeted by parties. The choices advance to a climax, the election. The winning party then begins the process of choosing spoils. These political choices must relate to the degree of victory achieved. If the winning party spoils are too little then it simply retreats from its victory; if its spoils are excessive then the balance of power may shift to the other party or may result in legal conflict, or war.

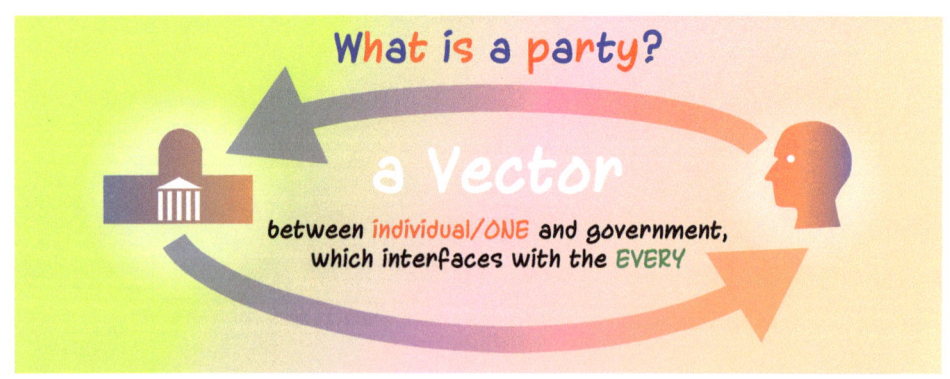

What is a party?

a Vector

between individual/ONE and government, which interfaces with the EVERY

What is the
EVERY/ONE Tug of War?

How is it reflected in The Democratic and Republican parties?

In December 1948 the General Assembly of the United Nations adopted the *Universal Declaration of Human Rights*. The United Nations had hoped for a common understanding of these rights and freedoms. A closer inspection of the articles demonstrates an admirable attempt. However, it is riddled with contradictions, lack of clarity and definition and, by necessity, culturally not unified. These articles do form a structure to select examples of values, value definitions, and method to achieve objectives promoting those values. Most Articles begin with "Everyone has the right to…". In English, this language immediately creates potential for paradoxes. In every considered situation, does "Everyone" focus on the "individual person"-one- or "all people" -every? In the context of conflicting choices, which focus takes priority? In either case, how is the right actualized?

How is this Universal Declaration of Human Rights important to the 2 party system?

This declaration provides a basis to consider examples within the relationship of the American election process, the evolving character of the two parties in the context of an overall model for human rights and values. The Democratic Party and Republican Party have patterns which may reflect their core responses to these concepts. The paradoxes and lack of clarity of these articles allow a wide range of deviation. They do establish a control mechanism to stage observations. Validity of the *Universal Declaration of Human Rights* for observational control purposes is supported by general acceptance worldwide.

Universal Declaration of Human Rights Preamble

Whereas recognition of the inherent dignity and of the equal and inalienable rights of all members of the human family is the foundation of freedom, justice and peace in the world,

Whereas disregard and contempt for human rights have resulted in barbarous acts which have outraged the conscience of mankind, and the advent of a world in which human beings shall enjoy freedom of speech and belief and freedom from fear and want has been proclaimed as the highest aspiration of the common people,

Whereas it is essential, if man is not to be compelled to have recourse, as a last resort, to rebellion against tyranny and oppression, that human rights should be protected by the rule of law,

Whereas it is essential to promote the development of friendly relations between nations,

Whereas the peoples of the United Nations have in the Charter reaffirmed their faith in fundamental human rights, in the dignity and worth of the human person and in the equal rights of men and women and have determined to promote social progress and better standards of life in larger freedom,

Whereas Member States have pledged themselves to achieve, in cooperation with the United Nations, the promotion of universal respect for and observance of human rights and fundamental freedoms,

Whereas a common understanding of these rights and freedoms is of the greatest importance for the full realization of this pledge,

Now, therefore, The General Assembly, proclaims this Universal Declaration of Human Rights as a common standard of achievement for all peoples and all nations, to the end that every individual and every organ of society, keeping this Declaration constantly in mind, shall strive by teaching and education to promote respect for these rights and freedoms and by progressive measures, national and international, to secure their universal and effective recognition and observance, both among the peoples of Member States themselves and among the peoples of territories under their jurisdiction.

Article 1

All human beings are born free and equal in dignity and rights. They are endowed with reason and conscience and should act towards one another in a spirit of brotherhood.

Cultural differences include age, gender, etc.

Article 2

Everyone is entitled to all the rights and freedoms set forth in this Declaration, without distinction of any kind, such as race, colour, sex, language, religion, political or other opinion, national or social origin, property, birth or other status. Furthermore, no distinction shall be made on the basis of the political, jurisdictional or international status of the country or territory to which a person belongs, whether it be independent, trust, non-self-governing or under any other limitation of sovereignty.

Article 2 confuses the rights of citizenship for different nations.

Article 3

Everyone has the right to life, liberty and security of person.

Article 4

No one shall be held in slavery or servitude; slavery and the slave trade shall be prohibited in all their forms.

Article 5

No one shall be subjected to torture or to cruel, inhuman or degrading treatment or punishment.

Article 6

Everyone has the right to recognition everywhere as a person before the law.

Article 7

All are equal before the law and are entitled without any discrimination to equal protection of the law. All are entitled to equal protection against any discrimination in violation of this Declaration and against any incitement to such discrimination.

"Incitement" may imply restriction of liberty (Article 3)

Article 8

Everyone has the right to an effective remedy by the competent national tribunals for acts violating the fundamental rights granted him by the constitution or by law.

Article 8 is a mission statement without clarity.

Article 9

No one shall be subjected to arbitrary arrest, detention or exile.

Article 10

Everyone is entitled in full equality to a fair and public hearing by an independent and impartial tribunal, in the determination of his rights and obligations and of any criminal charge against him.

Article 11

1. Everyone charged with a penal offence has the right to be presumed innocent until proved guilty according to law in a public trial at which he has had all the guarantees necessary for his defence.

"All the guarantees" is culturally variable.

2. No one shall be held guilty of any penal offence on account of any act or omission which did not constitute a penal offence, under national or international law, at the time when it was committed. Nor shall a heavier penalty be imposed than the one that was applicable at the time the penal offence was committed.

Article 12

No one shall be subjected to arbitrary interference with his privacy, family, home or correspondence, nor to attacks upon his honour and reputation. Everyone has the right to the protection of the law against such interference or attacks.

Conflict between speech liberty (Article 3) and "attacks on reputation"

Article 13

1. Everyone has the right to freedom of movement and residence within the borders of each State.

What right do states have to control their borders?

2. Everyone has the right to leave any country, including his own, and to return to his country.

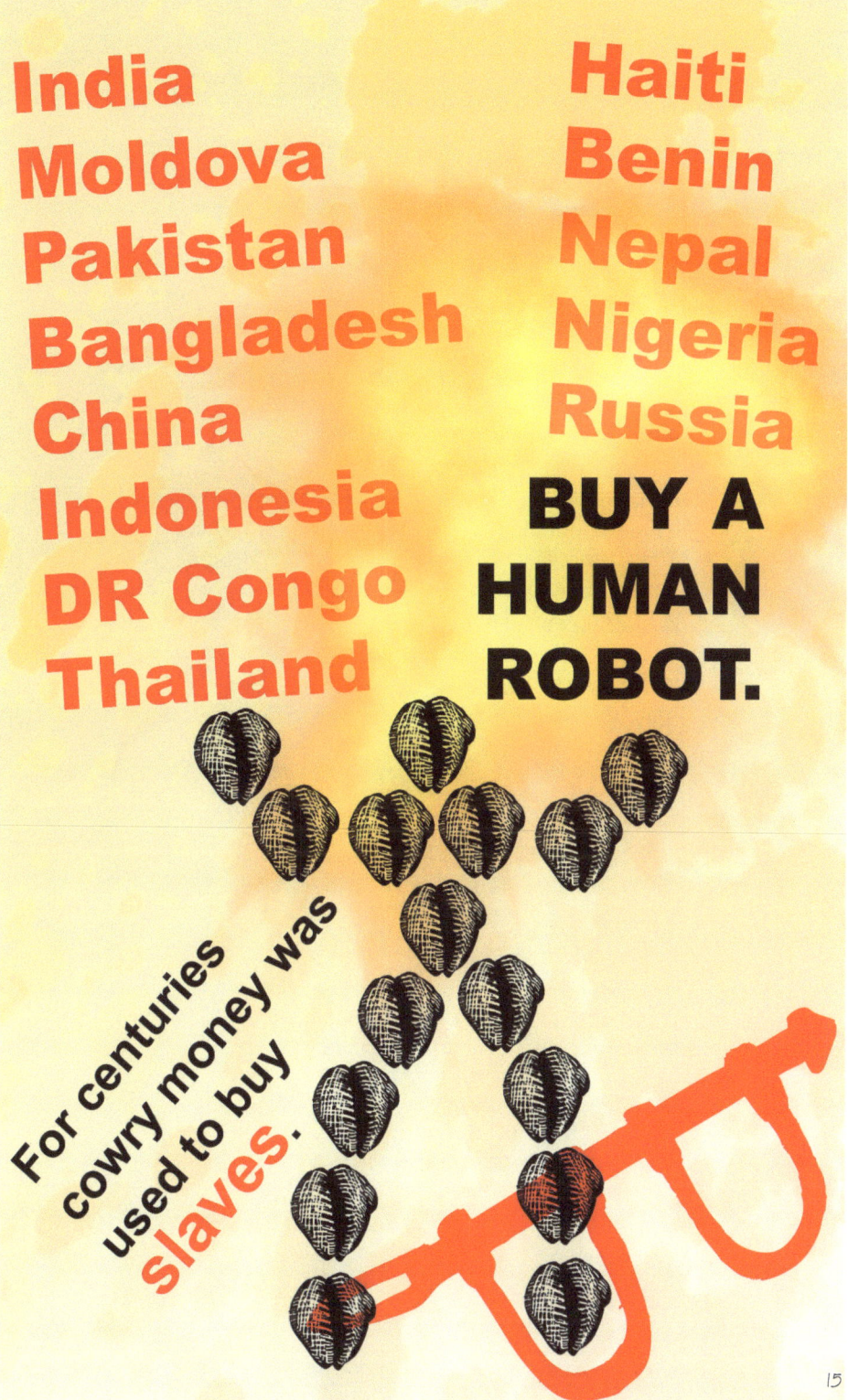

India
Moldova
Pakistan
Bangladesh
China
Indonesia
DR Congo
Thailand

Haiti
Benin
Nepal
Nigeria
Russia

BUY A HUMAN ROBOT.

For centuries cowry money was used to buy **slaves.**

Article 14

1. **Every**one has the right to seek and to enjoy in other countries asylum from persecution.

2. This right may not be invoked in the case of prosecutions genuinely arising from non-political crimes or from acts contrary to the purposes and principles of the United Nations.

How is this determined?

Article 15

1. **Every**one has the right to a nationality.

2. No **one** shall be arbitrarily deprived of his nationality nor denied the right to change his nationality.

Article 15 implies each person has the right to only 1 nationality.

Article 16

1. Men and women of full age, without any limitation due to race, nationality or religion, have the right to marry and to found a family. They are entitled to equal rights as to marriage, during marriage and at its dissolution.

Who defines marriage?

2. Marriage shall be entered into only with the free and full consent of the intending spouses.

3. The family is the natural and fundamental group unit of society and is entitled to protection by society and the State.

Article 17

1. **Every**one has the right to own property alone as well as in association with others.

2. No one shall be arbitrarily deprived of his property.

Article 18

Everyone has the right to freedom of thought, conscience and religion; this right includes freedom to change his religion or belief, and freedom, either alone or in community with others and in public or private, to manifest his religion or belief in teaching, practice, worship and observance.

Conflicts with Article 7

O Attic shape! Fair attitude! with brede
Of marble men and maidens overwrought,
With forest branches and the trodden weed;
Thou, silent form, dost tease us out of thought
As doth eternity: Cold Pastoral!
When old age shall this generation waste,
Thou shalt remain, in midst of other woe
Than ours, a friend to man, to whom thou say'st,
"Beauty is truth, truth beauty,"—that is all
Ye know on earth, and all ye need to know.

Ode on a Grecian Urn, Stanza 5
John Keats, A.D. 1820

In 1948, when the UN was adopting The Universal Declaration of Human Rights, the French architect Le Corbusier proposed THE MODULAR, a universal measure harmonious to human scale. This potential worldwide system reflected the abstracted concept of EVERYONE and ancient Greek concepts of mathematical beauty.

On these urns perfect Athenian men and women danced in black, white, gold and red glazes, around clay barriers to contents unknown. Encircling the urn, they represent a unified equality of beauty. Yet they danced and killed each other with equal disregard.

Today a smart phone can project a "selfie" photograph around a world encircled. Yet we dance and kill, remembering in pride that we are individuals. Our contents are not known, even to ourselves.

Article 19

Everyone has the right to freedom of opinion and expression; this right includes freedom to hold opinions without interference and to seek, receive and impart information and ideas through any media and regardless of frontiers.

Article 20

1. **Every**one has the right to freedom of peaceful assembly and association.

2. No **one** may be compelled to belong to an association.

Article 20 implies required group health insurance by state may violate international law.

Article 21

1. **Every**one has the right to take part in the government of his country, directly or through freely chosen representatives.

How does this apply to a federal republic?

2. **Every**one has the right to equal access to public service in his country.

3. The will of the people shall be the basis of the authority of government; this will shall be expressed in periodic and genuine elections which shall be by universal and equal suffrage and shall be held by secret vote or by equivalent free voting procedures.

Article 22

Everyone, as a member of society, has the right to social security and is entitled to realization, through national effort and international co-operation and in accordance with the organization and resources of each State, of the economic, social and cultural rights indispensable for his dignity and the free development of his personality.

This is a mission statement which must be defined by different cultures. Therefore there is no objective standard to qualify its achievement.

Article 23

1. **Every**one has the right to work, to free choice of employment, to just and favourable conditions of work and to protection against unemployment.

2. **Every**one, without any discrimination, has the right to equal pay for equal work.

Variables for "equal work" are too multiple to be clearly identified.

3. **Every**one who works has the right to just and favourable remuneration ensuring for himself and his family an existence worthy of human dignity, and supplemented, if necessary, by other means of social protection.

4. **Everyone** has the right to form and to join trade unions for the protection of his interests.

Article 24

Everyone has the right to rest and leisure, including reasonable limitation of working hours and periodic holidays with pay.

Article 25

1. **Everyone** has the right to a standard of living adequate for the health and well-being of himself and of his family, including food, clothing, housing and medical care and necessary social services, and the right to security in the event of unemployment, sickness, disability, widowhood, old age or other lack of livelihood in circumstances beyond his control.

2. Motherhood and childhood are entitled to special care and assistance. All children, whether born in or out of wedlock, shall enjoy the same social protection.

Article 26

1. **Everyone** has the right to education. Education shall be free, at least in the elementary and fundamental stages. Elementary education shall be compulsory. Technical and professional education shall be made generally available and higher education shall be equally accessible to all on the basis of merit.

2. Education shall be directed to the full development of the human personality and to the strengthening of respect for human rights and fundamental freedoms. It shall promote understanding, tolerance and friendship among all nations, racial or religious groups, and shall further the activities of the United Nations for the maintenance of peace.

3. Parents have a prior right to choose the kind of education that shall be given to their children.

Article 26 has potential conflict between the state, the U.N. and the parent.

Article 27

1. **Everyone** has the right freely to participate in the cultural life of the community, to enjoy the arts and to share in scientific advancement and its benefits.

Cultural differences confuse the meaning of "everyone."

Different cultures create a variety of concepts embodying the abstact idea of **EVERYONE**. These differences create conflicts in development of a unified world view of **EVERYONE**.

culture A

culture B

Cultural attempts to achieve world norms greatly vary and success is at different levels.

culture F

normative United Nations **EVERYONE**

culture C

culture E

culture D

Governments are created and then exist in relationship to the cultures they inhabit.

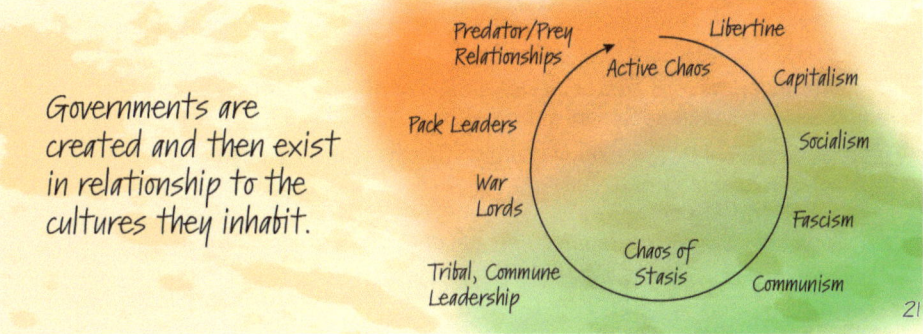

Predator/Prey Relationships

Libertine

Active Chaos

Capitalism

Pack Leaders

Socialism

War Lords

Fascism

Tribal, Commune Leadership

Chaos of Stasis

Communism

2. **Everyone** has the right to the protection of the moral and material interests resulting from any scientific, literary or artistic production of which he is the author.

Article 28

Everyone is entitled to a social and international order in which the rights and freedoms set forth in this Declaration can be fully realized.

Each person is unique, in his physical body, and in the context of his unique community. It is a different concept from the idealized "everyone". This leads to confusion.

Article 29

1. **Everyone** has duties to the community in which alone the free and full development of his personality is possible.

2. In the exercise of his rights and freedoms, **everyone** shall be subject only to such limitations as are determined by law solely for the purpose of securing due recognition and respect for the rights and freedoms of others and of meeting the just requirements of morality, public order and the general welfare in a democratic society.

3. These rights and freedoms may in no case be exercised contrary to the purposes and principles of the United Nations.

Article 30

Nothing in this Declaration may be interpreted as implying for any State, group or person any right to engage in any activity or to perform any act aimed at the destruction of any of the rights and freedoms set forth herein.

The United Nations Universal Declaration of Human Rights is the most widely translated document in history.

The Universal Declaration of Human Rights was adopted by the UN General Assembly on December 10, 1948. Eleanor Roosevelt chaired the **UDHR drafting committee**.
Source is: www.un.org/en/documents/udhr/history.shtml

Reprinted with permission of the United Nations

Why does the word
EVERYONE create paradox?

A cursory look at the word **EVERYONE** identifies one concept. In fact, it is two opposite concepts: **EVERY**, associated with "all" and **ONE**, implying the individual. This is a form of Dualism. The union in the word **EVERYONE** therefore creates a continual paradox. Which opposite is "real"; which is most important? If **EVERY** is most important, is **ONE** less important? If **ONE** is more important, is **EVERY** less important? If **EVERY** and **ONE** are of the equal importance, then how do we/I respond?

How do the Democratic and Republican parties currently perceive the paradox which arises in the word:

EVERYONE?

Language of the Democratic Party includes such phrases as "we are all in this together," "it takes a village to raise a child," "Americans believe," and "common good." The Republican Party uses such phrases as " individual rights," "freedom," "exceptionalism," and "excessive regulation." These are markers which point to a Democratic focus on community and a Republican focus on the individual; both are inherent in the word **EVERYONE**, the Dualistic word commonly used in the United Nations Universal Declaration of Human Rights.

How do "individual" and "community" affect different perceptions of "equal rights" for time sequences or distribution of resources and rights throughout any society?

The Democratic Party is very concerned with testing for an equal level of characteristic markers in a given community. To effectively control vectors toward equality, government regulation is seen as a positive social addition. The Republican Party is focused on the individual. It sees regulation by government as a barrier to personal actualization. Regulation is designed to limit deviation and, therefore, is negative. Increased regulation may stabilize equality of distribution over time but it must limit the free range of individual choice. Regulation maintains stability of that distribution. This conflict is central to Green\Red Tug of War. The Big Green Arrow of Time winds down and points to a peaceful equilibrium. It is a social corollary to the second law of thermodynamics. The end of history is the final value (stasis). Therefore each party sees the arrow of time differently. The arrow processes peacefully, or not; but it keeps history in motion as long as we have it and do not achieve complete equilibrium.

How does "**EVERYONE**" affect the concept of money?

Money, for this context, is defined as an in common mechanism universally used to quantify the value of all human transactions: intellect, physical, or things that constitute "products". The Democratic Party perceives "money" as a proper marker, or indicator to identify "**EQUALITY**" for given communities, the **EVERY** in "**EVERYONE**". The Republican Party perceives "money" as a tool to promote the actualization of "**FREE** will" in the individual, the **ONE** in "**EVERYONE**".

Conclusion

If the history of Presidential Elections creates some balance of wins between the two parties and their goals, then the game may continue in its present form. If stakeholders in either party believe the **EVERYONE** Tug of War can no longer function, that there is no longer the long term ability to win, or the game is rigged, then the game or parties may have to be modified or suppressed. If adaptations are not appropriate, then levels of **war** can result.

Sample stakeholders targeted by the **Democratic Party**

EVERY

- Unions
- LGBTQ
- Feminist groups
- Special interest grants
- Environmental issues
- Undocumented immigrants
- Colleges, teachers
- Racial minorities
- Pan nationalism
- Equality issues

The party is a loose coalition of targeted groups with diverse objectives that may or may not be in common. The party is based on the intense allegiance of target group members to the group's primary objective that is supported by the party. That objective may be the singular glue binding the voter to the party.

Sample stakeholders targeted by the **Republican Party**

ONE

- Budgeting, Financial, Debt and taxes concerns
- National Security
- Social Conservative Personal Issues
- Over Regulation Concerns

A coalition of targeted groups or individuals with related multiple objectives, having in common elements, characterized by multiple glue bondings.

Reciprocal Action Tug of War in Campaign for Capturing the Votes

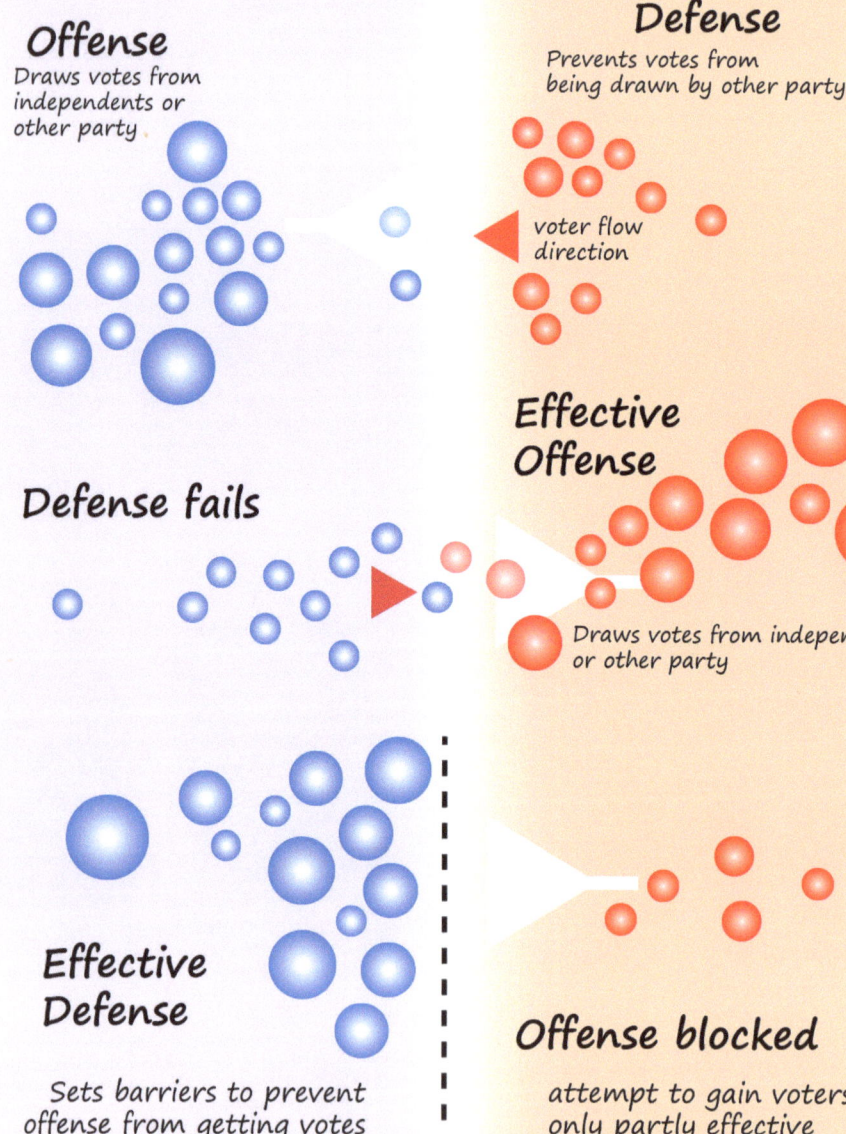

Offense
Draws votes from independents or other party

Defense
Prevents votes from being drawn by other party

voter flow direction

Defense fails

Effective Offense
Draws votes from independents or other party

Effective Defense
Sets barriers to prevent offense from getting votes

Offense blocked
attempt to gain voters only partly effective

Objective: to win votes and expend resources of opposite side

Stakeholders and Equality:
Democrats

Integration of the party is founded in an in common value, equality. Unchecked, this attribute points toward stasis and regulation to prevent community deviations. However, the current party coalition is dependent on allegiance by very specific groups with tailored objectives. Intensity is a reward for narrowness, but there may not be broad social relevance. Paradoxes in the party's different support groups' positions abound and may not be resolved. These paradoxes, caused by one issue links to the party, can trivialize unity. Some personalities may change party vote based on this trivialization of common factors and paradoxes.

If the voter believes his primary self interest is the same as community targeted objectives he will vote Democratic. The voter who identifies himself in a social standing below what he believes to be the standard for the overall community may seek wealth supplements provided by government.

(Article 23, United Nations Human Bill of Rights)

"Victim-hood" is the political derogatory concept.

Stakeholders and Freedom:
Republicans

Integration of the party is founded in an in common value, individual freedom. Unchecked this attribute points toward domination by the fittest. Major target groups in this party are tied together with in common objectives. Vagueness is a condition necessary for this broad social relevance with multiple issues. This may lead to less intense commitments than those by voters with a major primary issue, as in the Democratic coalition. Personalities which focus on one issue may choose parties based on intensity in regard to that issue.

The voter who identifies his productivity above what he perceives the standard for the overall community may vote Republican. He believes his self-interest contrasts with community targeted objectives of Democrats because he is handing his earned wealth to the community without his consent.

(Article 27, United Nations Human Bill of Rights)

"GREED" is the political derogatory concept.

Stakeholder Morale and Commitment in the Democratic Party

Stakeholder Morale and Commitment in the Republican Party

Because this loose coalition is dependent on allegiance to very specific groups with very intensely felt, but tailored, objectives, its composition and morale is fluid. Paradoxes in party's position abound. Individual voters may change parties because of these conflicts.

Major target groups in this party are tied together with in common objectives which are characterized by multiple issues.Commitment is less divided by category than the Democratic Party. One issue personalities may change party vote based on that election's specifics.

Marketing Rule:

Party brand must actualize the voter's will at some level. This may be accomplished through support for a significant party objective or a party spokesperson that the voter strongly identifies as a representative of his personality, will, or his SELFNESS.

COMMUNITY ISSUE VOTERS
EVERY

UNDECIDED VOTERS

PERSONAL FREEDOM VOTERS
ONE

Committed voters are ideological or see a high level of contrast between parties.

Independents, undecided, and changeable voters see low transitional differences in the parties or perceive value conflicts in themselves or party objectives.

Committed voters are ideological or see a high level of contrast between parties.

Time Sequence of Tug of War Campaign

Predisposing factors of party in power (Time 1):

- Appropriate spoils and their usage
- Economics and social environment
- Leadership effectiveness and trust
- Before campaign evaluations
- Maintain support of previous stakeholders

Predisposing factors of party out of power:

- Satisfaction/dissatisfaction with government
- Long or short term party goals
- History of current administration
- Popular trust
- Support of previous stakeholders and addition of new stakeholders

Enabling factors of party in power (Time 2):

- Network to build support groups
- Public satisfaction with current political, economic, and social environment
- Before campaign evaluations and planning
- Finance
- Surprise events

Enabling factors of party out of power:

- Network to build support groups
- Public dissatisfaction with current political, economic, and social environment
- Before campaign evaluations and planning
- Finance
- Surprise events

Reinforcing factors of party in power (Time 3):

- Effective follow-up of all campaign tactical events
- Effective usage of spoils promotes positive perception of party by voters after election victory
- Stakeholder primary objective conflicts

Reinforcing factors of party out of power: (Time 3)

- Effective follow-up of all campaign events
- Monitoring of party in power's usage of spoils
- Effective and appropriate counter of elected power

Effective executive power by controlling party gives supremacy to that party. Perception of ineffective government gives supremacy to the out of power party. Evaluation of campaign method, finance, and defense/ offense therefore must be planned on realistic evaluations.

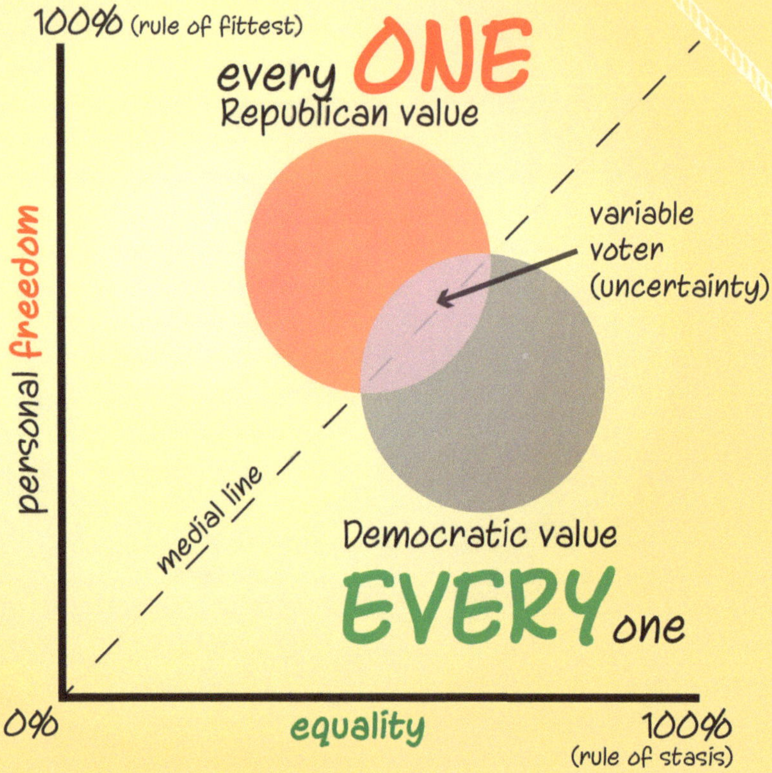

100% (rule of fittest)

every **ONE**
Republican value

personal *freedom*

variable
voter
(uncertainty)

medial line

Democratic value
EVERYone

0%   equality   100%
(rule of stasis)

Power Swings

personal freedom

TIME 1

equality

personal freedom

TIME 2

equality

TIME 3

equality

Fluctuation in controlling party power over time
preserves the election game and prevents chaos.
Game winners reciprocate dominance.

Who is the President?

LIKABILITY

The president must reflect qualities and emotions that the voter feels because the President represents and is therefore **THE VOTER.**

STATESMAN

As head of state the President stands for the country as the warlord, the elected prince of state. He is the **EAGLE.**

Effective Administration

The President must have the skills to be chief executive, work with Congress, and speak for his party. He must be an **EFFECTIVE POLITICIAN.**

EVERY / ONE?

The campaign is like a grand animal fair. The candidates are paraded. Voters measure strength, agility, and stamina to determine performance. Do they have good conformation, character, and poise to be statesmen? We measure against our standards. Are they of good breeding quality? Are they likeable? Perhaps they would even make a good pet? What are the characteristics of your favorite animal? What are your personal standards? The voter makes his own choice, but he must choose within the **EVERYONE** paradox because the paradox is contained in the position of President itself.

Executive Power:
Life Cycle Feedback Loop for Party

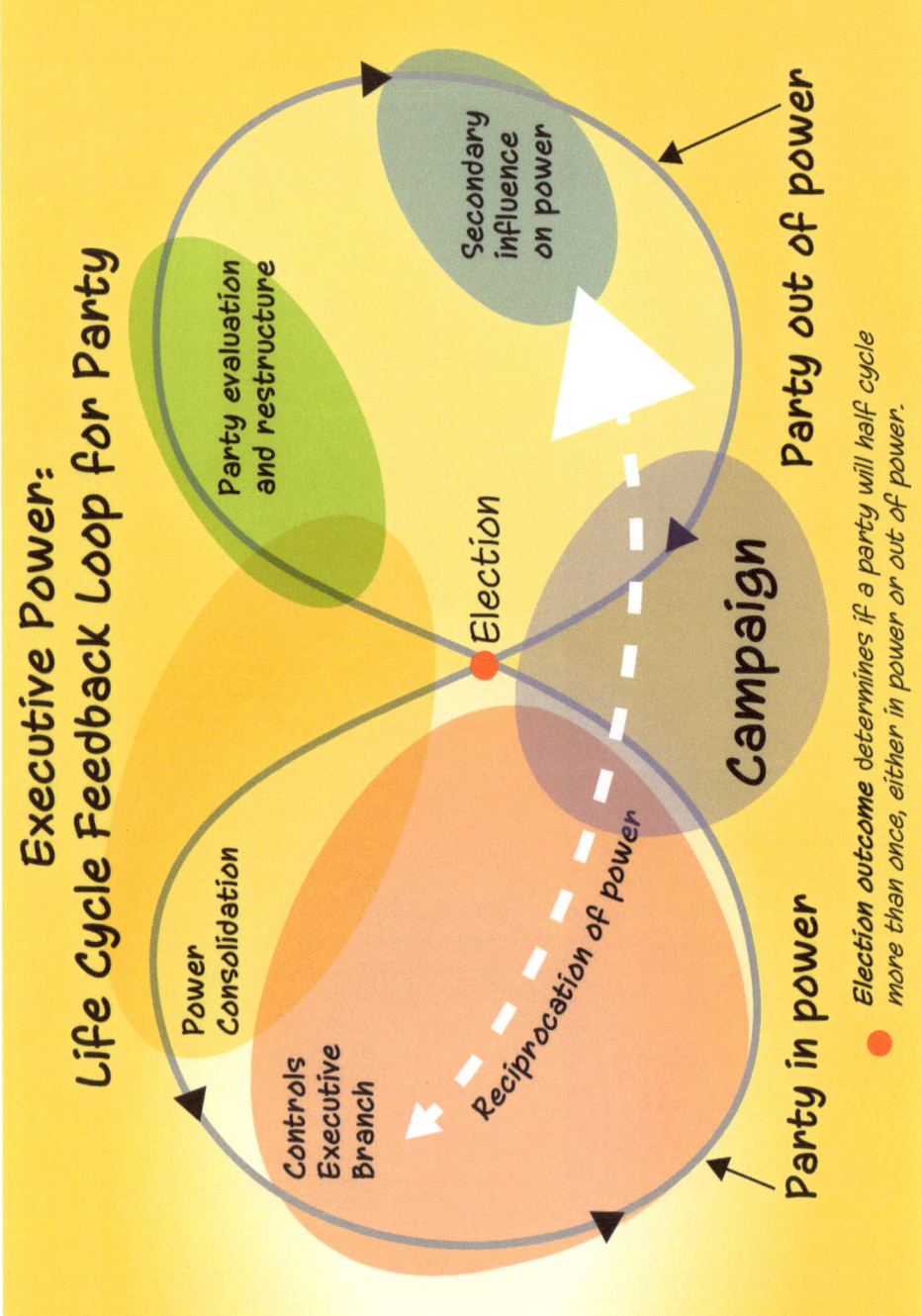

Party evaluation and restructure

Secondary influence on power

Election

Party out of power

Campaign

Power Consolidation

Reciprocation of power

Controls Executive Branch

Party in power

● Election outcome determines if a party will half cycle more than once, either in power or out of power.

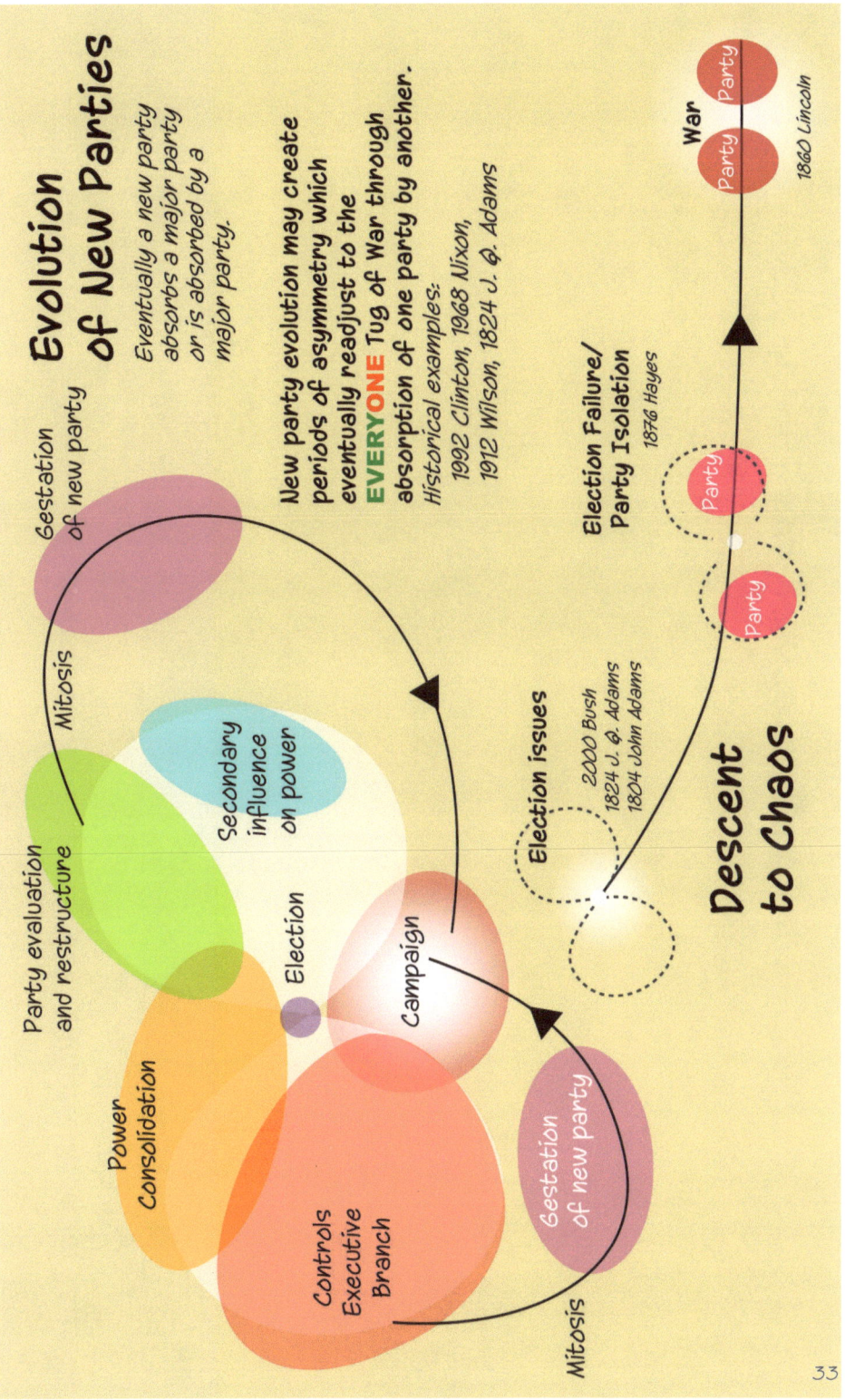

Evolution of New Parties

Eventually a new party absorbs a major party or is absorbed by a major party.

Gestation of new party

Mitosis

Party evaluation and restructure

Power Consolidation

Secondary influence on power

Election

Campaign

Controls Executive Branch

Gestation of new party

Mitosis

New party evolution may create periods of asymmetry which eventually readjust to the **EVERYONE** Tug of War through absorption of one party by another.
Historical examples:
1992 Clinton, 1968 Nixon, 1912 Wilson, 1824 J. Q. Adams

Election Issues
2000 Bush
1824 J. Q. Adams
1804 John Adams

Election Failure/ Party Isolation
1876 Hayes

Party

Party

Descent to Chaos

War

Party   Party

1860 Lincoln

The Campaign Process of the TUG of War

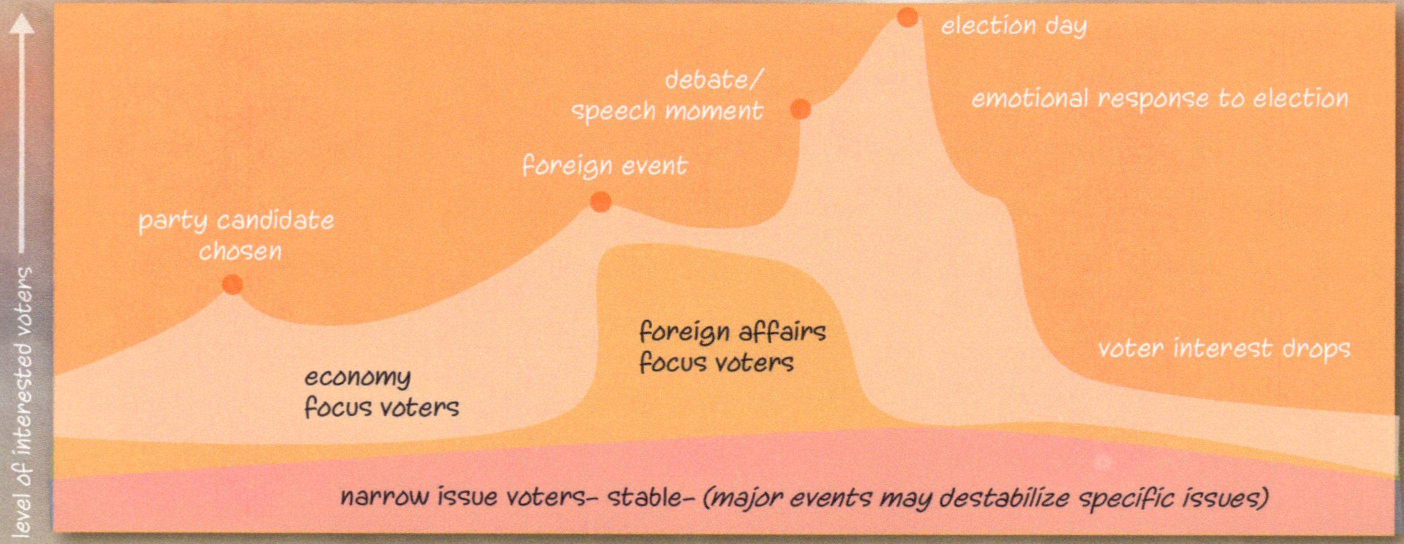

level of interested voters ←

- party candidate chosen
- economy focus voters
- debate/ speech moment
- Foreign event
- election day
- emotional response to election
- foreign affairs focus voters
- voter interest drops
- narrow issue voters– stable– (major events may destabilize specific issues)

Scenario model: time lapse of party campaign with voter focus interests

The EVERYONE Paradox:
Intellect or feeling?

Intellect

Feeling

Each person's voting decision is a unique combination of intellect and feeling. The heart and mind may be reconciled, or not reconciled. Eventually we act. We respond according to our SENSIBILITY.

Politics and EVERYONE

Socialist,
Communist

Diverse
Issue,
Narrow issue
Democrats

Independents

Diverse
Issue,
Narrow issue
Republicans

Libertarian,
Survivalist

The duel between the concepts EVERY/ONE creates perpetual choices, both for the individual and for the community. If the process is measured in seconds for the individual, or in a relatively long time within groups (consensus), then we can describe them as fitting on a continuum between the extremes of "every" and "one". That it is not perceived as evaluation does not mean that the decision process doesn't take place. This is the most basic of animal responses; the foundation is in both voluntary and involuntary nervous systems. Higher level thought has specified this exchange into community (every)-personal (one). The political party is a means to extend this exchange into the civil arena. Each person may reflect the balancing of community and the personal differently in a variety of community contexts: family, friends, social groups, religion, and in the expression of politics. To voice and affirm personality in a political context, one must eventually vote for a candidate, usually Democrat or Republican.

Duration of Choice

CONCEPT: Size of community X time of process = potential political and social impact

DURATION: national elections and legislative decisions

DURATION: local, county and state decisions

DURATION: social and neighborhood decisions

DURATION: family, friends, small groups decisions

quick personal decisions

Duration of time for reciprocations and evaluation of EVERY/ONE paradox

How do individuals perceive
EVERYONE?

The personal space of the individual is a diameter of about 6 feet. As distance increases the concept of personal relationship decreases. The individual is surrounded by a background of people who become the vague "EVERYONE". We spend our time scanning back and forth both the sensory and conceptual space between "I" or "ONE" and the "EVERY". Like the predator or the prey we detect MOVEMENT first. At this point we switch focus from "ONE" to the perceived "EVERY".
We imagine one image, one concept: EVERYONE.
In fact, there are two extreme poles: EVERY / ONE

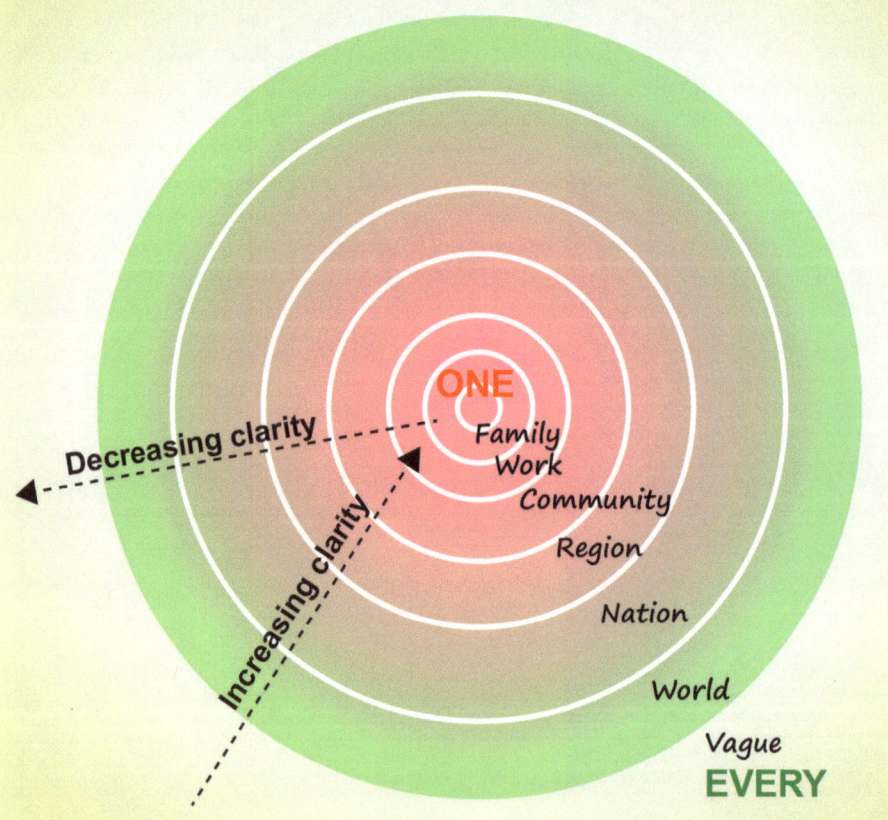

ONE
Family
Work
Community
Region
Nation
World
Vague
EVERY

Decreasing clarity

Increasing clarity

Santa Claus

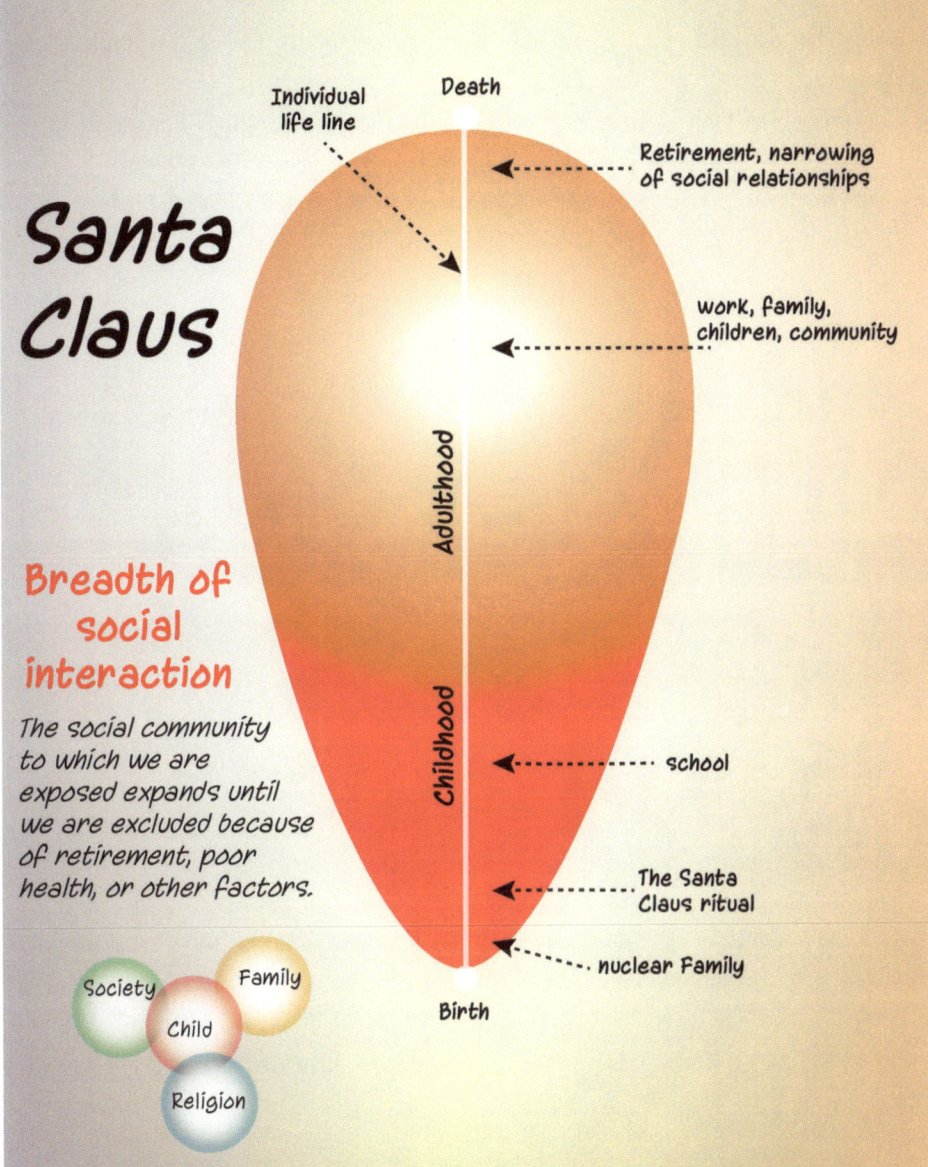

Individual life line

Death

Retirement, narrowing of social relationships

work, family, children, community

Adulthood

Childhood

school

The Santa Claus ritual

nuclear Family

Birth

Society

Family

Child

Religion

Breadth of social interaction

The social community to which we are exposed expands until we are excluded because of retirement, poor health, or other factors.

The **Santa Claus** ritual introduces the child to the social contract. If successful, the child learns these rules:
- Good behavior may be rewarded
- Rewards and lack of rewards may come from society, as well as the family
- Interactions with other children prove life is not just. The child learns rewards and punishment are not equal for all children.
- Each child has personal wants, needs, and feelings.

Religious Topological (Modality) Groups

Definition: Religion is the organizing methodology individuals use to relate life's separate experiences and observed phenomena. The intent is to achieve personal order and identity in response to multiple external experience stimuli.

EVERY   ONE

Traditional Religions with Deity (feedback)

community   ← *Power exchange* →   church   ← *Power exchange*   God/Gods = one

Individual = one

Secular Religions (feedback)

community   ← *Power exchange* →   state   ← *Power exchange*   Controlling document/s = one

Individual = one

Cults

Power flow

every and person-hood = the same   control oligarchy   cult leader = one

Theocracy

Power flow

every and person-hood = the same   control oligarchy   God/Gods = one

Dictatorship

Power flow

every and person-hood = the same   state   Strongman/men = one

(Cults, Theocracies, and Dictatorships demonstrate little reciprocation of power)

Victim-hood points to chaos.

ADULTS must learn the rules:
- Good behavior may be rewarded.
- Society may give rewards.
- Neither of the first two may happen.
- Each individual develops a different set of personal wants, needs, and resolution of those needs.

ADULTS who do not learn these rules develop envy and resentment, potentially a strong component of elections.

Individuals who do not learn these rules develop envy and resentment, potentially a strong component of elections.

Dissention

EVERYoneEVERYoneEVERYone   everyONEeveryONEeveryONE

I am everyman, therefore I am entitled to equal status and material goods under the law. This is because I am EVERYman.

I have performed well above others and should be rewarded accordingly. I resent giving up my rightful share to those less worthy. This is because I am everyONE.

Self-perceived victims process information from routed perspective.

Campaign appeal to victim-hood elevates emotions and builds momentum toward intense polarization and conflict. It points to a chaotic destruction of the game: potential war.

It destroys empirical examination of issues. It creates vilification.

Geographic Constants and Variables

Constant:

Natural geography is dominantly constant. Exceptions include the Suez and Panama canals, England to France tunnel, and major water developments such as the Aswan Dam in Egypt.

Variables:

- Location and movement of cultural, national, and ethnic groups

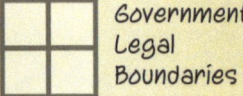 Governmental Legal Boundaries

 Racial, age, language, narrow issue variables

 Ethnic, cultural, class variables overlap and are in continuous flux.

- Education curriculum, content, and effectiveness within geographic area
- Community religion and habits
- Standard of living, chance for change of status, equality factors within natural geographic area
- Speed of travel and communications technology

Variables with conceptual obstacles:

- legal boundaries or regulation (includes financial regulation)
- educational curriculum modifications

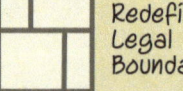 Redefining Legal Boundaries

- regulation for factors which address very specific issues or promote change for specific social markers, legal language

The more isolated the variable the easier it is to identify processes to change it. The paradox is that simplicity in modifying the variable may be inverse to its real effect on a geographic area, to background. Short term campaigns and party success ,therefore, may not lead to long term effectiveness.

Example: In the 1960's rivers flowing into the Aral Sea were diverted for the Soviet Union's cotton irrigation. Focus on one issue created an ecological catastrophe. Today the Aral Sea is 10% of its former size.

MALE CITIZENS VOTED IN ANCIENT ATHENS AND THE ROMAN REPUBLIC.

WOMEN FIRST VOTED:

1755 CORSICAN REPUBLIC
1881 ISLE OF MAN
1893 NEW ZEALAND
1902 AUSTRALIA
1913 NORWAY
1917 RUSSIA
1918 CANADA
1920 UNITED STATES

Concept: Historical Expansion of Franchise
as a part of Population (U.S. example)

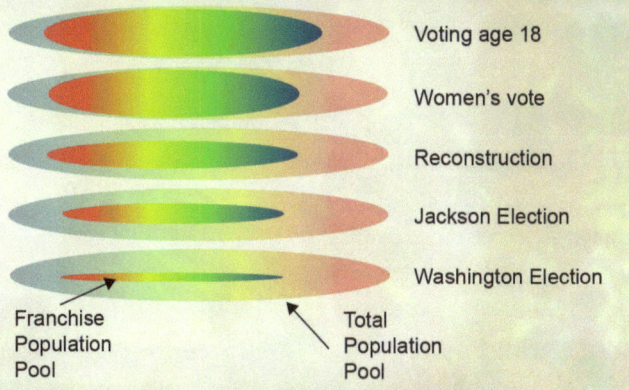

Voting age 18

Women's vote

Reconstruction

Jackson Election

Washington Election

Franchise Population Pool

Total Population Pool

Demographic changes in voters creates ongoing party modification and values. Is a larger voter pool necessarily more representative of the entire population?

Why do Utopias fail?

All defined geographic political units trade, exchange culture and citizens from other geographic political units; therefore, the character and membership of constituency changes in time. Then different geographic units modify prehension of each other.

EVERYone Utopia

Any Utopia designed to create a purely equal society must regulate any deviation from set norms identifying "equality", control tolerances for time sequenced deviations and limit external prehension. They eventually must create an **oppressive stasis** of cultural characteristics and behaviors.

everyONE Utopia

Any Utopia designed to create a pure individual "freedom" will result in domination by the fittest with ultimate suppression of the weak, an oppression with unpredictable change.

A democratic society cannot be a **Utopia** because the constant conflict between EQUALITY and PERSONAL FREEDOM leads to a perpetual TUG OF WAR. This causes an organic flux of development, maturation, and decay of the relative posture in the strength of these two perspectives. The success of **Democracy** is appropriate frequency and intensity of this exchange. This organic nature allows the system to adjust to changes in its constituency and culture over time. This organic nature makes the process messy and, in short term evaluation, awkward, like the personal lives of EVERYONE.

MORBIDITY
in a Democracy

EVERYONE Tug of War issues descending to Conflict

Outbreak Conflict Examples

- Haymarket Riot- Chicago- 1886
Event recognized throughout the world – International Workers Day-May 1
- especially in the old Soviet Union and Cuba
-multiple coal and mining Union and management conflicts, 1870's -1920's
- civil rights violence events, Eisenhower Administration, Johnson Administration, 1957-1968
-Weathermen bombing at Haymarket Square, Chicago, 1969, 1970
Oklahoma City Bombing 1995
Fort Hood terrorism 2009

Epidemic Conflict Examples

-San Elizario Salt War, Texas, 1877
- multiple border area conflicts 1915-1916

Single Pandemic Conflict

-Civil War- Reconstruction-
Compromise of 1877, Samuel Tilden vs. Rutherford B. Hayes,
Failure of National Election Process 1861-1877

Issues in these conflicts identified in the United Nations Declaration of Human Rights include:
Articles 1-10, 13, 15, 16,17, 20, 21, 23, 24, 26

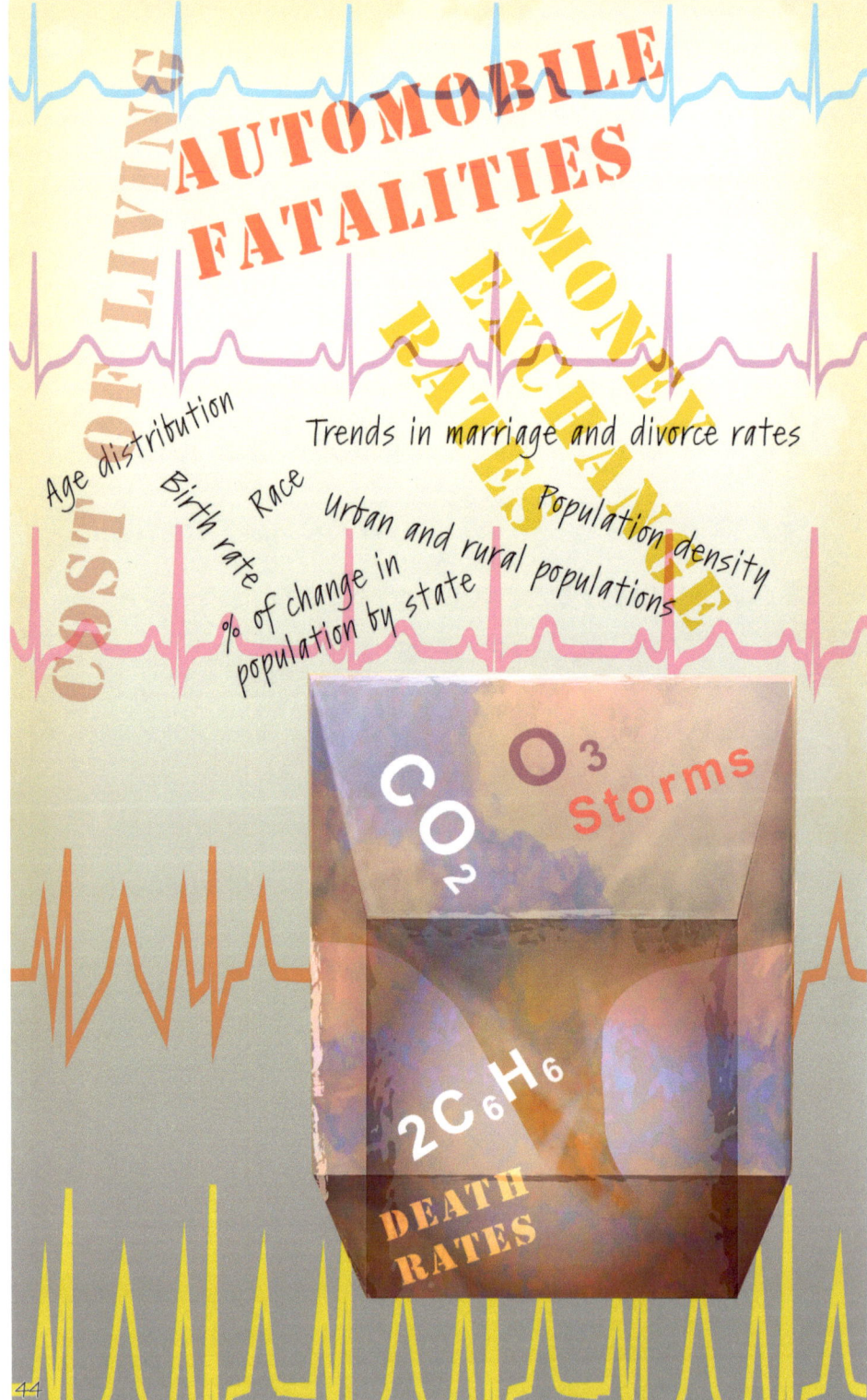

<u>Definition:</u> Markers are signals. They allow us to perceive environmental changes with effectiveness and efficiency.

Examples of markers include:

MONEY, UNITS OF EXCHANGE: gold, shells, silver, bonds, rice, stocks, carbon credits

Fair Exchange:

quantity money A X value of money A = quantity money B X value of money B

HUMAN SUFFERING (NATURAL DISASTERS, WAR): casualties

EQUAL Exchange:

Casualty rate A X value of cultural stakes A x value of citizens A =
Casualty rate B X value of cultural stakes B x value of citizens B

BIOLOGICAL AND CHEMICAL:

traditional public health markers, morbidity, mortality, heavy metal, ozone, etc.

Carbon Credits:

New technology allows communities and governments to control biological and chemical variables utilizing markers of their choosing. Hydrocarbon credits offer control of CO_2. This pandemic regulation would expand the concept of community worldwide. It has both scientific and religious implications in the Second Law of Thermodynamics, stasis and the death of history, entropy. Factors under consideration to evaluate the EVERY/ONE paradox are these: real evironment effect, effect on personal FREEDOM, definition of community, background and unintended effects, good design, and appropriate pretesting.

National Health Panels:

Information and data exchange offers complete regulation by the executive branch over biological functions of EVERY/ONE. Does this provide good care for the most citizens or does it inhibit freedom,? This is the paradox. This is not unlike casulties in war: the value of each citizen relates to the number of people receiving health care. The value of an individual soldier relates to the quantity of total casualties in war.

Novelty and Perception

Sensory perception of predator species (top of food chain) and prey (lower in food chain) all rely on immediate identification of difference. Examples include sound (sudden noise, change of pitch or timbre) and vision (motion, sharp color or value contrasts). Predation within the species focuses on size (power) and gender. These characteristics are channeled in the perceptions of higher level animals, including man. The common denominator for both predation and defense is novelty of the condition perceived (contrast). The number of related sensory experiences by the perceiving animal is a decisive factor in acknowledgement, identification, and emotional response to the sensory data perceived. Increased experience creates a background to compare event data. This decreases identification of events and issues as being novel. Intensity is diminished as an experience is related to a broader background.

As in animals, novelty and perception affect responses by targeted voters in political campaigns. Specifically focused issues create a narrow social relevance, more contrast. Their reward is perceived novelty and intensity. The Democratic Party attracts this type of voter. For example, this may account for specifically younger voters supporting narrow issues. The Republican Party has developed more generalized issues. This may reduce intensity and contrast. At the same time, there is broader social relevance. The belief that people become conservative as they grow older only to defend accumulations of power and wealth may be overly cynical. The more an animal experiences, the less likely it is to judge an event or datum as novel. They are increasingly likely to relate the issue or event to past experiences and thus to a background. Contrast may become transitional. The ability to make adequate judgment, or discernments, often accounts for survival in the animal kingdom. This may account for Republican Party support by older voters.

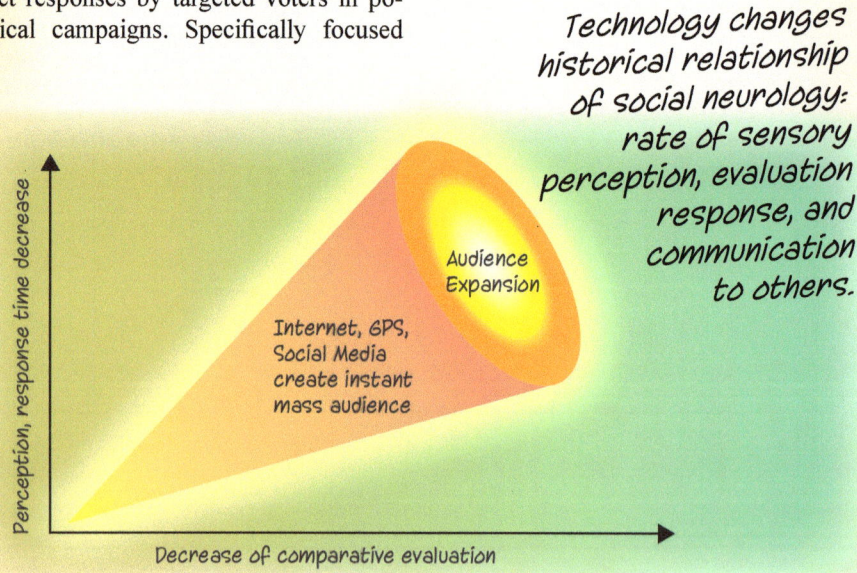

Technology changes historical relationship of social neurology: rate of sensory perception, evaluation response, and communication to others.

Perception, response time decrease

Audience Expansion

Internet, GPS, Social Media create instant mass audience

Decrease of comparative evaluation

Technology Perception and Response

The end of the American Civil War is often dated from the Battle of Appomattox, dated April 9, 1865. The last Battle was on May 26, 1865, at Brownsville, Texas, six weeks later. On June 10, 1962, the Telstar satellite was launched and transmitted live images from London. The geometric increase of data is now expressed instantaneously to mass audiences all over the world, creating a world neurological system. The components of this sensory pattern in most of man's history were stimuli-emotional and intellectual evaluation-response. World surveillance systems, GPS, GIS, and the internet with social media create instant distribution and response to data. This instant exchange of stimuli creates an expectation of faster and faster reciprocation of a stimuli-respond-stimuli-respond pattern, not unrelated to addiction. The advantage of new technology has the positive effect of allowing appropriate, fast, effective response to situations requiring them (example: early detection of disease, hurricanes). The disadvantage is that the routed desire to respond quickly affects the quality of decision-making. This includes improper evaluation of cause and effect and potential collateral damage for actions taken. As this stimuli-response pattern accelerates, it may contract decision making to " feelings". This has a profound effect on the design of political campaigns. The narrow issue is adaptable to sound bites and 10 second ads. It is more easily " Twittered". This medium is supreme for an accelerated behavior pattern. It does not function well to identify background and relational information. The adaptation of newspapers to lower reading levels, devolving of standard English, and the number of character limits on Twitter are examples. They adapt thought process to media, not media to the thought process. Because information is presented in small bites to a mass audience, cultural unity and understanding of issue background relationships will break down. An entire group of citizens may develop basic thought and conceptual processes channeled by the limitations of instant media.

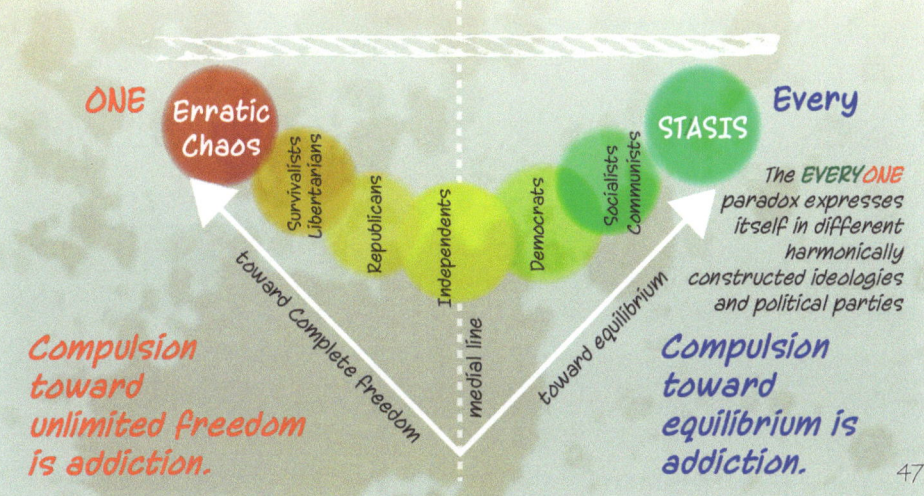

ONE Erratic Chaos — Survivalists, Libertarians, Republicans, Independents, Democrats, Socialists, Communists — STASIS Every

toward Complete Freedom — medial line — toward equilibrium

The EVERYONE paradox expresses itself in different harmonically constructed ideologies and political parties

Compulsion toward unlimited freedom is addiction.

Compulsion toward equilibrium is addiction.

The Future: What IF?

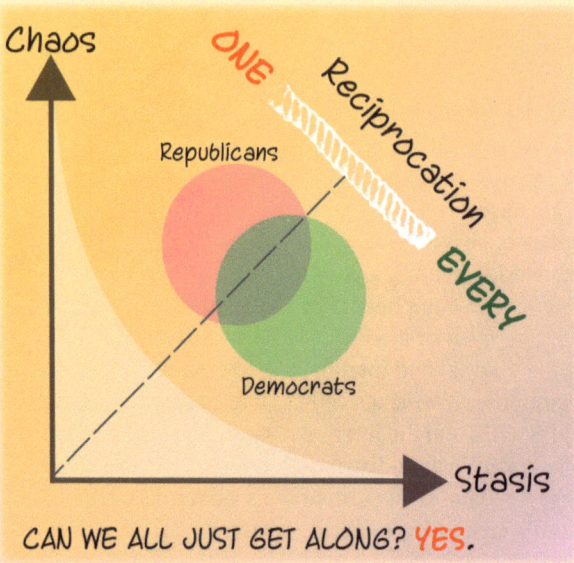

CAN WE ALL JUST GET ALONG? YES.

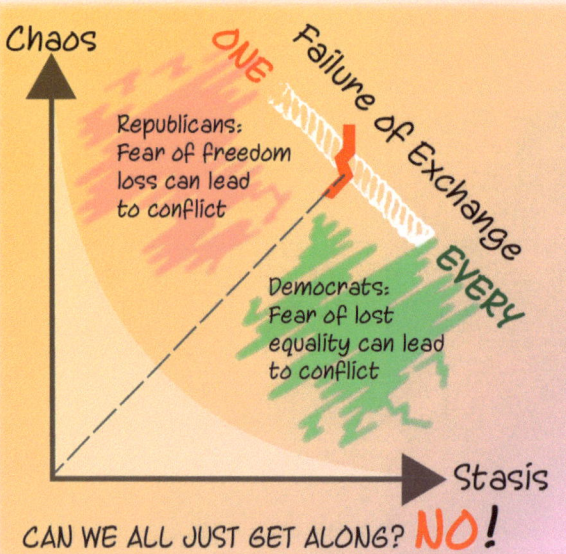

CAN WE ALL JUST GET ALONG? NO!

System Failure can be repaired by nations or parties that evaluate variations in values and processes. Alternatives include emergence of new parties and change in the total legal structure and/or process. Conflict or war may result if these repairs are not made.

Solution Variations: values and parties

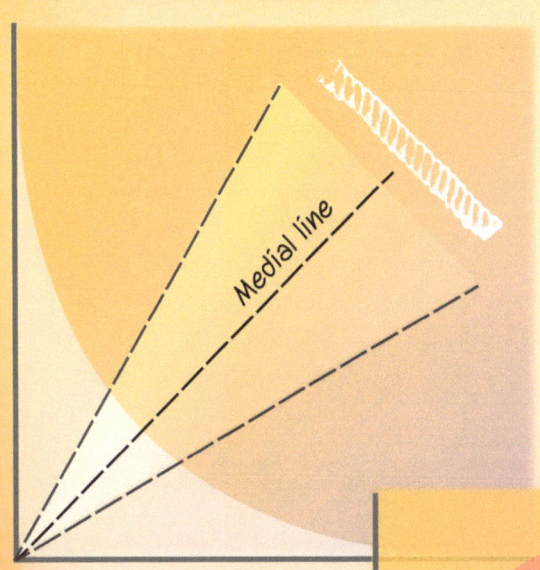

A

Culture changes concept of the medial values between **EVERY** and **ONE** in continuing reciprocation.

B

Parties reconstruct to form new reciprocation and interchange.

C

Parties reconstruct to form new interchange.

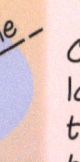

Culture changes locational concept of the medial values between **EVERY** and **ONE**, and then continues reciprocation.

The constantly changing future will impose unexpected choices which require opening the doors of our minds just to survive.

Geographic Variations

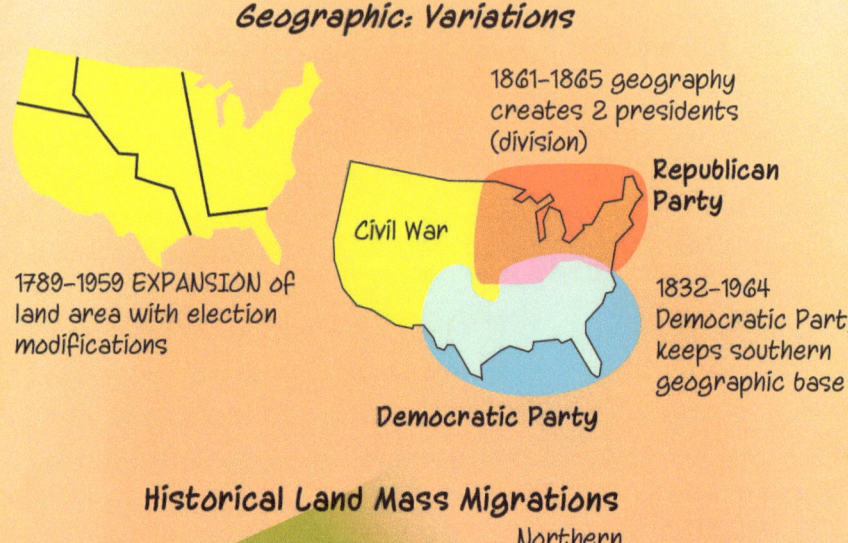

1861–1865 geography creates 2 presidents (division)

Republican Party

Civil War

1789–1959 EXPANSION of land area with election modifications

1832–1964 Democratic Party keeps southern geographic base

Democratic Party

Historical Land Mass Migrations

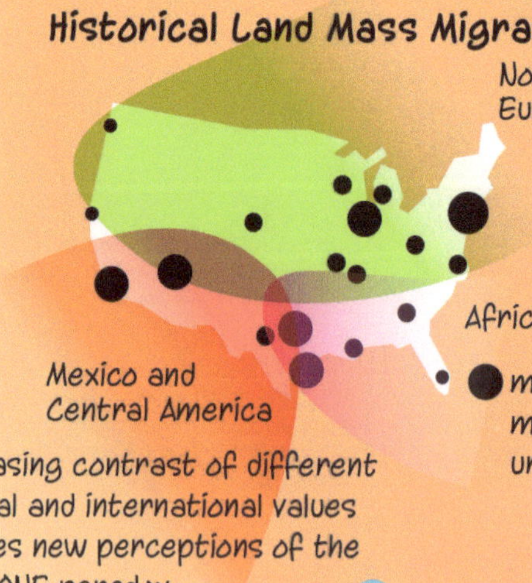

Northern European

African

Mexico and Central America

modern multicultural urban centers

Increasing contrast of different cultural and international values creates new perceptions of the EVERYONE paradox

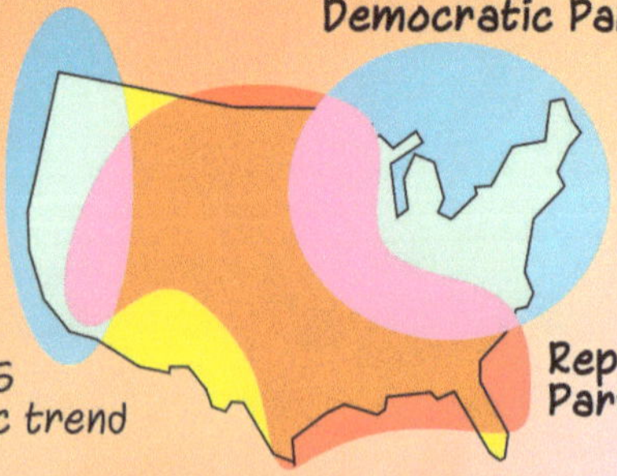

Democratic Party

2000–2015 Geographic trend

Republican Party

Geographic locations create different perspectives for each person concerning the meaning of EVERYONE.

Peru

India

Paris

New York City

The future changes the relationship of population and resources in regard to inventions, technologies, and imagination. **EVERYONE** must choose modes of adaptation. How well we adapt will define **EVERYONE**'s quality of life.

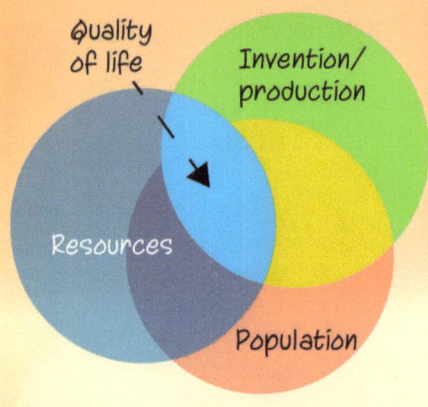

Quality of life

Invention/production

Resources

Population

The intersect of population, resources and invention/production decides the potential for quality of life. How we use them is our social and political choice.

Alternate Futures

Population – Time$_2$

Smaller work force or changes in age distribution may diminish external power.

Population – Time$_1$

Population – Time$_2$

Larger population requires more resources and/or effective invention/production.

Population Change

Resources – Time$_2$

Decrease in resources requires decrease in population and/or effective invention/production to prevent loss of quality of life.

Resources – Time$_1$

Resources – Time$_2$

Larger population requires more resources and/or effective invention/production,

Resource Change

Time changes of element relationships that affect the EVERYONE Tug of War

Present

3 Futures

Resources

Invention

Population

Future 1

Future 2

Future 3

Alternate choices to sustain quality of life

- Fewer resources require loss of population, increased invention, or external expansion (war)
- Increased population requires increased resources and/or invention, or external expansion (war)

AND/OR:

- Equalizations of loss of standard of living throughout population
- Attempt to create climate to increase invention
- Create mix which preserves existing EVERYONE TUG OF WAR

International relations are controlled by these same elements.

Scoring an Improvisational Visual Music for the Tug of War

The conceptual vagueness of language and our choice of society's markers create an inadequate scientific investigation of the relationship of EVERY to the ONE. Although extremely helpful these inquiries are handicapped because they are limited by our definition and identification of variables. Additionally, by the time variables are identified and quantified their actual location and characteristics have changed. Thus, art and science can both be components in more fully understanding the conceptual paradox of EVERYONE.

Political notation shows exposition and resolution in concert with development.

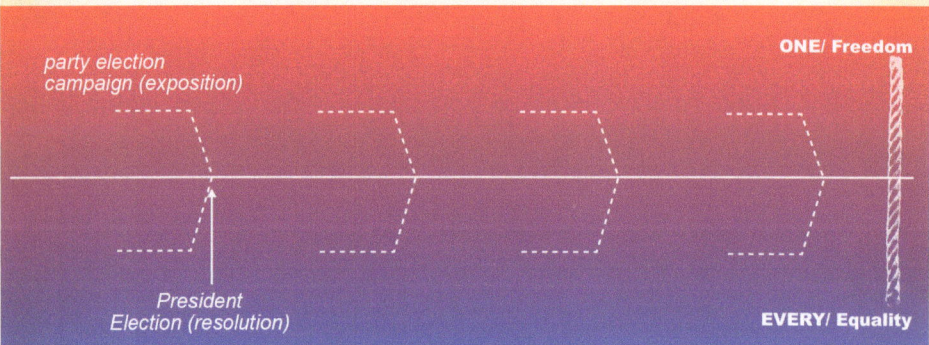

Actual government process (development) continuous (exception: total war)

The following are series of VISUAL TIME SCORES which represent my personal EXPRESSIONIST interpretation of EVERYONE sampled from the past. Each individual person may create his own scores. These SCORES may also focus on specific subgroups or identified categories. For example, in addition to major parties in Presidential elections, internal party conflicts at all government levels could be interpreted within the EVERYONE Tug of War. All interpretations would be different because of each person's perception. Even so, realistically considered evaluations would have much in common.

John C. Fremont, first Republican candidate for President, crusaded against chattel slavery. This would have expanded the concept of EVERY. Slavery supporters contended any restriction of slavery would restrict personal FREEDOM. This would have diminished the right of what was considered EVERY in a culture that did not include blacks and chattel slaves as equals.

The Democrat, James Buchanan, won the 1856 election but did not solve the conflicts concerning slavery in Kansas, Missouri, and Nebraska.

The fragmentation of political parties helped engineer the election of the first abolitionist Republican President. The conflict between the different concepts regarding EVERY and the subsequent different interpretations of FREEDOM created the Civil War.

Reconstruction with military occupation in Southern states continued until 1877. Southern racial conflict regarding the relationship of EVERYONE became expressed in "Jim Crow" laws. These laws were designed to identify two EVERYs, one black, one white. Not only limiting the FREEDOM of Blacks, segregation also placed limits on White FREEDOM in racial interactions.

Between 1865 and 1877 the Thirteenth, Fourteenth, and Fifteenth Amendments to the United States Constitution were adopted to redefine the relationship of EVERY to ONE. The Civil Rights Act in 1964 and the Voting Rights Act of 1965 may be understood as an extenuation of the Civil War.

Civil War

Jefferson Davis, C.S.A.
(elected by C.S.A. Constitutional Convention of Southern Democrats)

Democratic Party
(split between two candidates)

Constitutional Union

Democratic Party

Know Nothings

Republican Party
(John C. Fremont, candidate)

Democratic Campaign

Republican Campaign

Union
(Republican Party)

Democratic Party

Republican Party

ONE/ Freedom

EVERY/ Equality

1856
James Buchanan
(Democratic Party's popular sovereignty approach to slavery)

1860
Abraham Lincoln elected
(Republican), U.S.A.

1864
Lincoln reelected,
1865 killed

1868
Grant elected, promotes
15th Amendment

In 1888 the school student Ella Askins opened her modern geography book to learn about the world beyond her mountains in eastern Pennsylvania, only a few miles from the site where living adults had defeated the Army of Virginia at the Battle of Gettysburg, thus securing freedom for Southern slaves. Concerning the races of man Mitchell's New Intermediate Geography read:

The great family of mankind - although descended from Adam and Eve - by being spread over the surface of the earth and subjected to the varieties of climate, and from other causes, has been divided into several distinct races, differing in color, form, and features, and in mental characteristics also.

How many races of men are there?
There are five races: the Caucasian, or White race; the Mongolian, or Yellow race; the African, or Black race; the Malay, or Brown race; and the American; or Red race.

What is said of the Caucasian race?
The Caucasian race includes the civilized nations of Europe, and America, and is superior to the rest in mind, courage, and activity.

Of the Mongolian race?
The Mongolian race comprises many of the nations of Asia; its best specimens are found in China and Japan.

Of the Black race?
The African, or Black race, is found in all parts of Africa except on the northern coast; and in America, where they have been brought and domesticated.

Of the Malay race?
The Malay race is found in most of the islands of the Pacific Ocean, and also in the Peninsula of Malacca, in Asia.

MALAYAN

MONGOLIAN

CAUCASIAN

AFRICAN

AMERICAN

VAN INGEN-N.Y.U.S.A.

Of the Red race?
The American, or Red race, is found in America. The people of this race are commonly called Indians, and include all the tribes of the Western Continent, except the Esquimaux at the North, who belong, with the Laplanders, to the Mongolian race.

Mitchell's New Intermediate Geography, A System of Modern Geography for the Schools and Academies, by S. Augustus Mitchell, Published by E. H. Butler and Co.,1888, printed in Philada., Penn.

NOTE: The "Races of Man" are defined by geographic relationship to the targeted student in Eastern United States and to the culture of both the student and the author of the text. This personal relationship is characteristic worldwide in defining different valued levels of **EVERYONE**.

1960-1968, End of the Civil War by Other Means (*a Southern Election Perspective*)

in the 1960 Election the South votes Democratic

The 1960 election is the last election when the post reconstruction Solid South electors vote for a Democratic president. A post Reconstruction history of segregation, focus on individual state authority, and Republican President Eisenhower's support for Supreme Court rulings regarding school integration helped elect John F. Kennedy president. Black voters were disenfranchised by Poll Tax.

In the 1964 Election the South flips to Republican

Overt support by the John F. Kennedy administration's Attorney General Robert F. Kennedy and later support by President Johnson for black civil rights contrasted with Republican Senator Barry Goldwater's support for State Rights. This flipped Louisiana, Mississippi, Alabama, Georgia, and South Carolina to vote Republican in 1964.

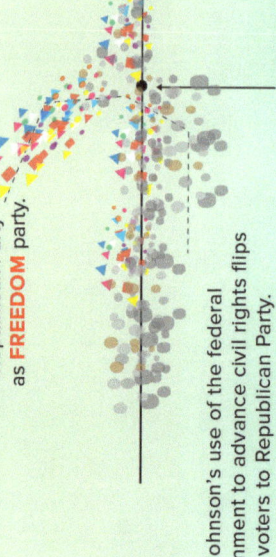

White voters view Democratic Party as **FREEDOM** party.

ONE/
Freedom

EVERY/
Equality

Republican Party

Eisenhower support of Warren Supreme Court rulings concerning segregation promoted Solid South votes for the Democratic Party.

Kennedy elected

White voters view Republican Party as **FREEDOM** party.

ONE

EVERY

Johnson's use of the federal government to advance civil rights flips voters to Republican Party.

Johnson elected

In the 1968 Election the South votes American Independent, ending Southern Democratic Party support since Reconstruction and the Civil War

Engagement of Democratic President Johnson in the Vietnam War created a national environment for the election of a Republican president. Additionally, President Johnson's strong support for civil rights laws and his introduction of Medicare, Medicaid and the War on Poverty required the extension of federal power over the individual state. Arkansas, Louisiana, Mississippi, Alabama and Georgia voted for George Wallace of the American Independent Party which promoted State Rights and continuation of segregation. Changes in party platform positions broke the ritual pattern of block Democratic voting in the South. Increased Black voting supported Democratic Party.

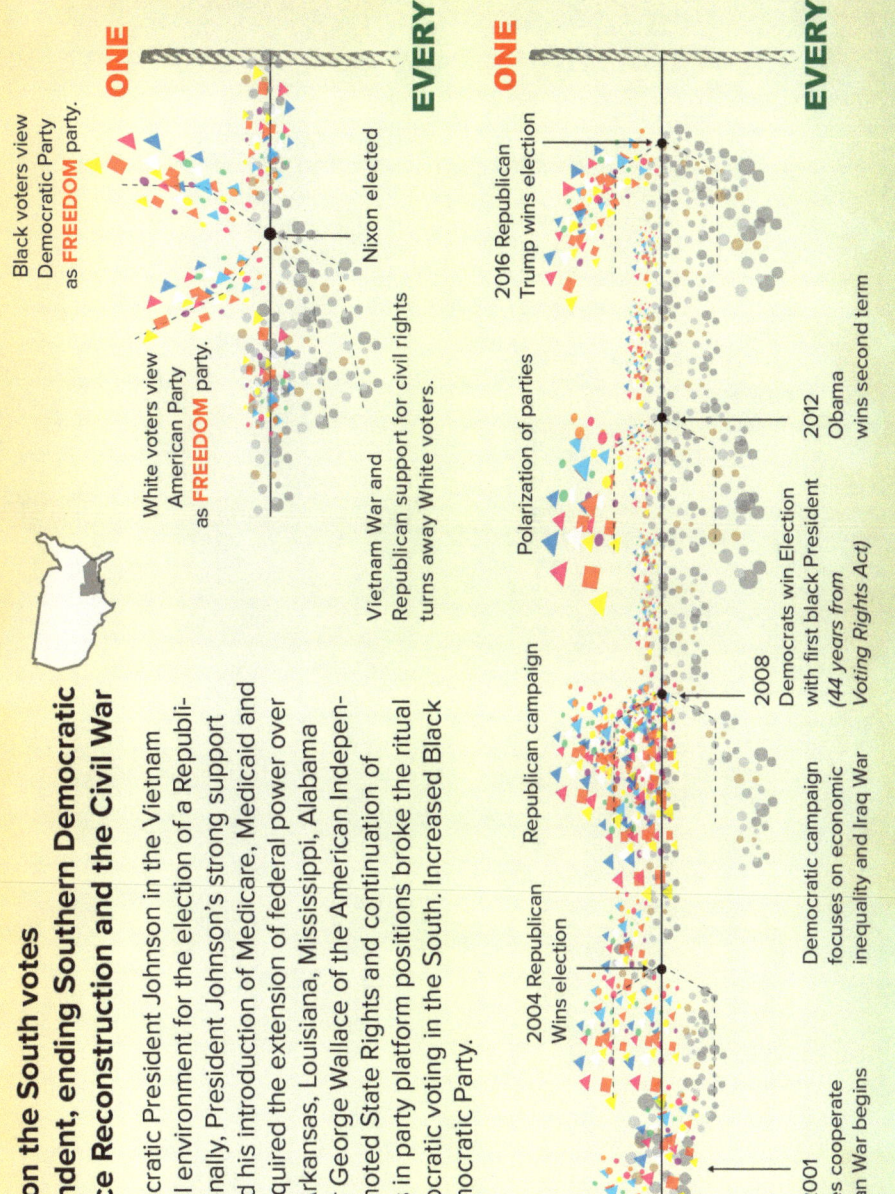

Black voters view Democratic Party as **FREEDOM** party.

White voters view American Party as **FREEDOM** party.

Nixon elected

Vietnam War and Republican support for civil rights turns away White voters.

2016 Republican Trump wins election

Polarization of parties

2012 Obama wins second term

Republican campaign

2008 Democrats win Election with first black President *(44 years from Voting Rights Act)*

Democratic campaign focuses on economic inequality and Iraq War

2004 Republican Wins election

9-11-2001 Parties cooperate Afghan War begins

ONE

EVERY

ONE

EVERY

POST 2000
EVERYONE
TUG OF WAR

Creating Classifications of EQUALITY or Multiple Sets of EVERYS

EQUALITY: In each person's life the paradox of **EVERYONE** is mitigated with levels of attachment. Personal liberties are extended by us to others with whom we are most attached, we most love. The more personal the relationship the more **liberties** extended to the other person. At the same time the natural **FREEDOM** of the other person is expected to match the **liberties** extended. This creates understanding relationships based on **EQUAL** worth. Conflicts arise when parties in any relationship conceive a different set of **liberties** to **FREEDOM** or a different level of **EQUALITY**.

Mutual acceptance by different parties concerning the levels of personal relationship and the balance of **liberties** and **FREEDOM** can lead to an effective relationship. Any misunderstanding or disagreement in the terms of the relationship exchange can lead to conflict.

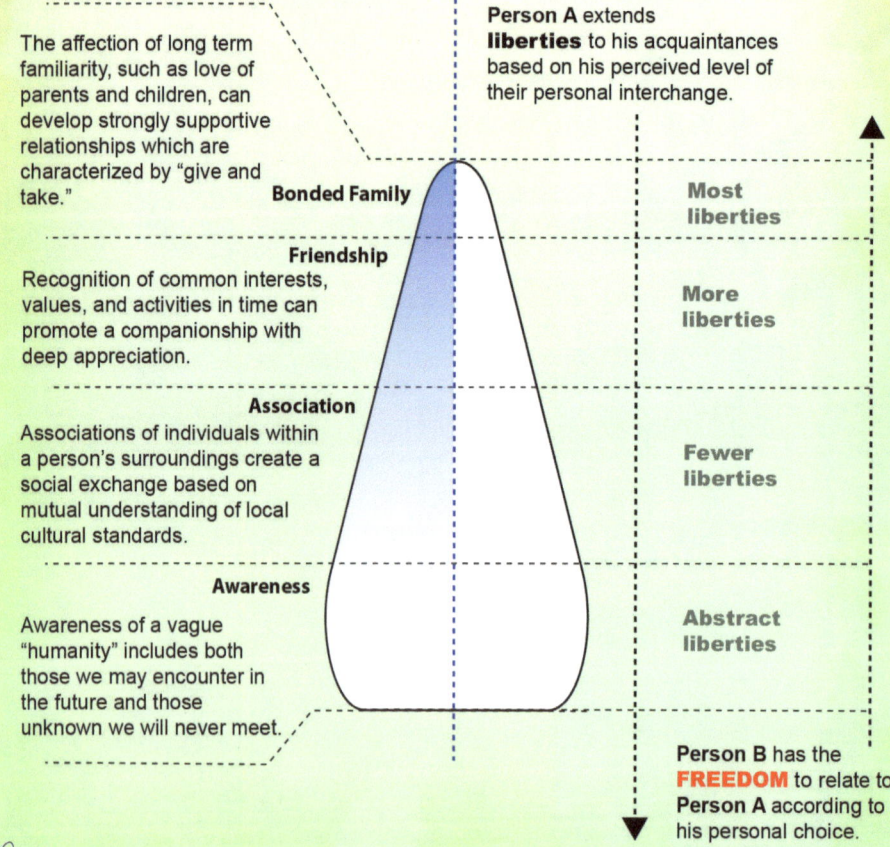

The affection of long term familiarity, such as love of parents and children, can develop strongly supportive relationships which are characterized by "give and take."

Recognition of common interests, values, and activities in time can promote a companionship with deep appreciation.

Associations of individuals within a person's surroundings create a social exchange based on mutual understanding of local cultural standards.

Awareness of a vague "humanity" includes both those we may encounter in the future and those unknown we will never meet.

Person A extends **liberties** to his acquaintances based on his perceived level of their personal interchange.

Bonded Family

Friendship

Association

Awareness

Most liberties

More liberties

Fewer liberties

Abstract liberties

Person B has the **FREEDOM** to relate to **Person A** according to his personal choice.

Classifications of EQUALITY in Organizations, Governments and Culture

All human cultures organize groups which mimic the behavior of their creators, individual people. Since these artifical groups are patterned from human behavior and are controlled by men, governments will also mitigate the **EVERYONE** paradox with classifications of **EQUALITY**. Classification methods have included race, location of birth, sex, religion, age, wealth, education, economic value, prenatal/postnatal, intelligence, handicapped status, class status at birth, citizenship, language, and physical characteristics. Different cultures, using different criteria and standards, develop these class structures for **EVERYONE**.

Mutual acceptance by different classes or nations concerning the level of relationship and the balance of **liberties** and **FREEDOM** can lead to an effective relationship. Any misunderstanding or disagreement in the terms of the relationship exchange can lead to conflict or war.

Class of leadership with common interests, and long term familiarity, develop strong methodologies to retain power and promote their ideas.

Nation A extends **liberties** to citizens or to other nations based on a perceived level of the **EQUALITY** interchange.

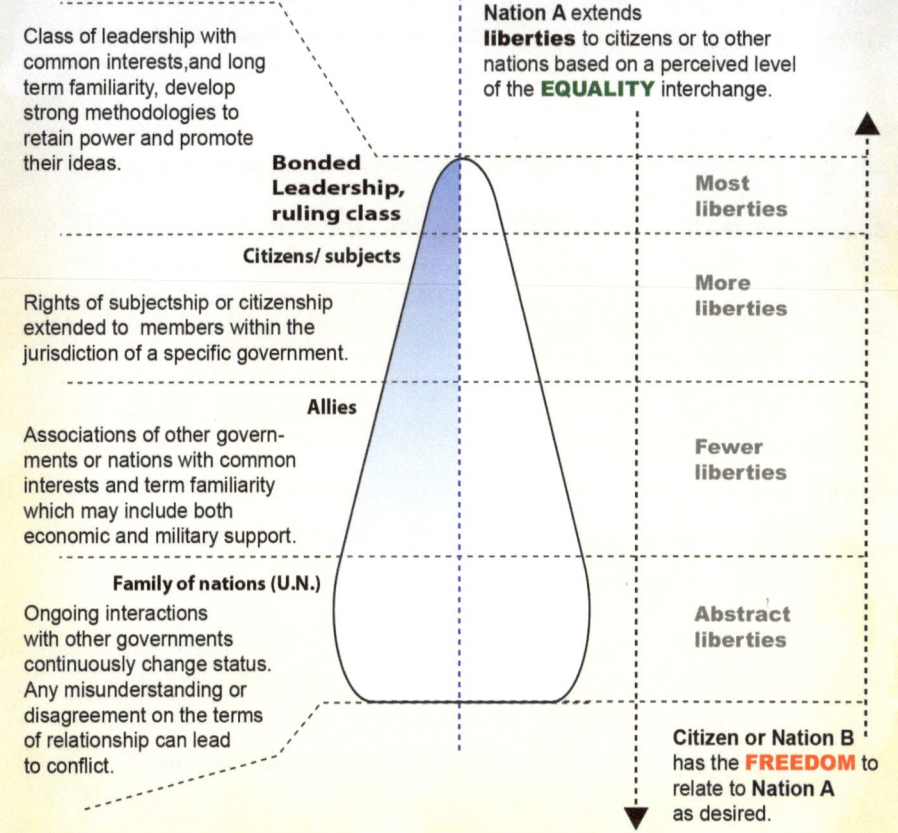

Bonded Leadership, ruling class

Most liberties

Citizens/ subjects

More liberties

Rights of subjectship or citizenship extended to members within the jurisdiction of a specific government.

Allies

Associations of other governments or nations with common interests and term familiarity which may include both economic and military support.

Fewer liberties

Family of nations (U.N.)

Ongoing interactions with other governments continuously change status. Any misunderstanding or disagreement on the terms of relationship can lead to conflict.

Abstract liberties

Citizen or Nation B has the **FREEDOM** to relate to **Nation A** as desired.

United Music Republic Game

Republics often elect heads of state through an election system which recognizes the sovereignty of the membership of sub states. Thus, the electoral vote system recognizes the power and will of each state in electoral votes which express the aggregate will of the people of that individual sub state. Then the electoral process represents both the geographic will of a sub state and the popular will of its people. When popular votes are accrued for the nation alone voting reflects a singular state, not a federal republic of sub states.

The **United Music Republic Game** requires 2 players, 1 die and a score sheet to tally points each player makes on his die throw. Player 1 chooses to play the **FREEDOM** PARTY or **EQUALITY** PARTY. Then he throws the die and tallies points for the first state *(Folk)*. Player 2 throws die and tallies his opposition points for the first state

(Folk). Players alternate until all 10 musical states are completed.

Total all 10 squares for each player to arrive at a popular vote for each party *(sum total of votes tallied for each player)*. This represents voting in a nation with centralized power. The winner simply has the most popular votes.

For electoral votes the player with the highest number cast for each state *(example: Folk)* receives the electoral votes for that state *(splits if tied on the 2 squares)*. Total the electoral votes for each state and the **FREEDOM** or **EQUALITY** Party that receives the highest number of electoral votes wins.

Often the same party wins both the popular and electoral vote. Sometimes a party will win the electoral vote and lose the popular vote.

Why choose a popular vote for the United Music Republic Game?

I just like all music and listen to everything– not just any one type. Everybody uses a guitar. As long as I can play a guitar I will play any type of music.

Why choose an electoral vote for the United Music Republic Game?

I just like Hiphop and don't listen to anything else. I want Hiphop to be represented the best way it can be. I just love it. A slide trombone. It's mellow, man. I'm jazzed.

United Music Republic Game

Electoral or Popular? Who wins the game?

55 – State's Electoral Vote

| 55 | 20 | 25 | 15 | 8 | 10 | 6 | 3 | 4 | 38 |

F6 F5 F4 F3 F2 F1
E1 E2 E3 E4 E5 E6

Begin election

Result

Folk Rap Hiphop Jazz Disco Gospel Rock Pop Blues Swing

FREEDOM

EQUALITY

63

An **EVERYONE** Time Score for the Tug of War for election of a President is very much like the Tug of War that takes place in our minds when we make our individual decisions. We consider both the effect on us, and others around us. Thus we qualify who **EVERYONE** of value is to us and what our actions may cause. All unorganized or organized groups engage in a similar process. For this reason the process of election in government is a reflection of the organic process of choice made by **EACH PERSON**. It repeats our own nature. Over and over we confront the **PARADOX**.

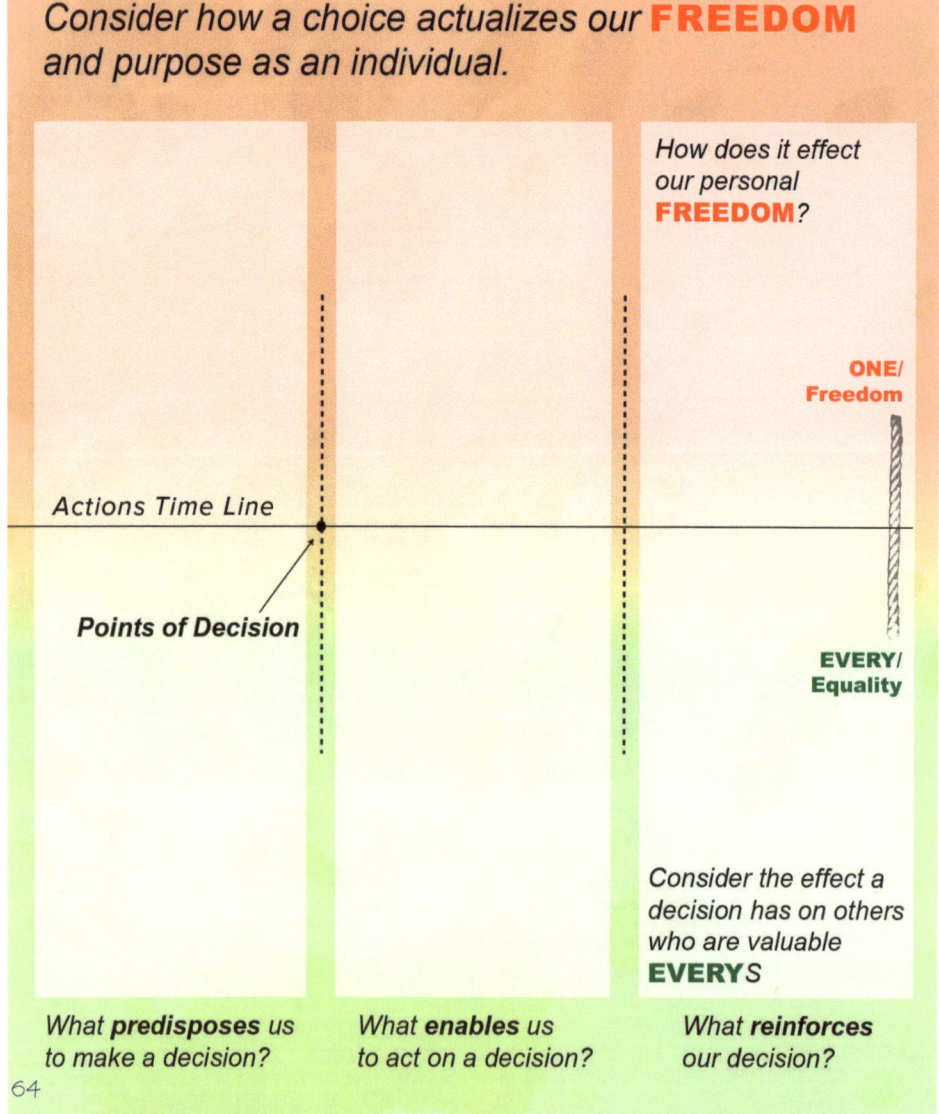

Consider how a choice actualizes our **FREEDOM** *and purpose as an individual.*

How does it effect our personal **FREEDOM**?

ONE/ Freedom

Actions Time Line

Points of Decision

EVERY/ Equality

Consider the effect a decision has on others who are valuable **EVERY**S

*What **predisposes** us to make a decision?*

*What **enables** us to act on a decision?*

*What **reinforces** our decision?*

Create Your Own Classification of EQUALITY

EQUALITY: In each person's life the paradox of **EVERYONE** is mitigated by levels of attachment. What are your levels of attachment? To whom are they offered? Each person has the **FREEDOM** to make these choices himself. What markers do you use?

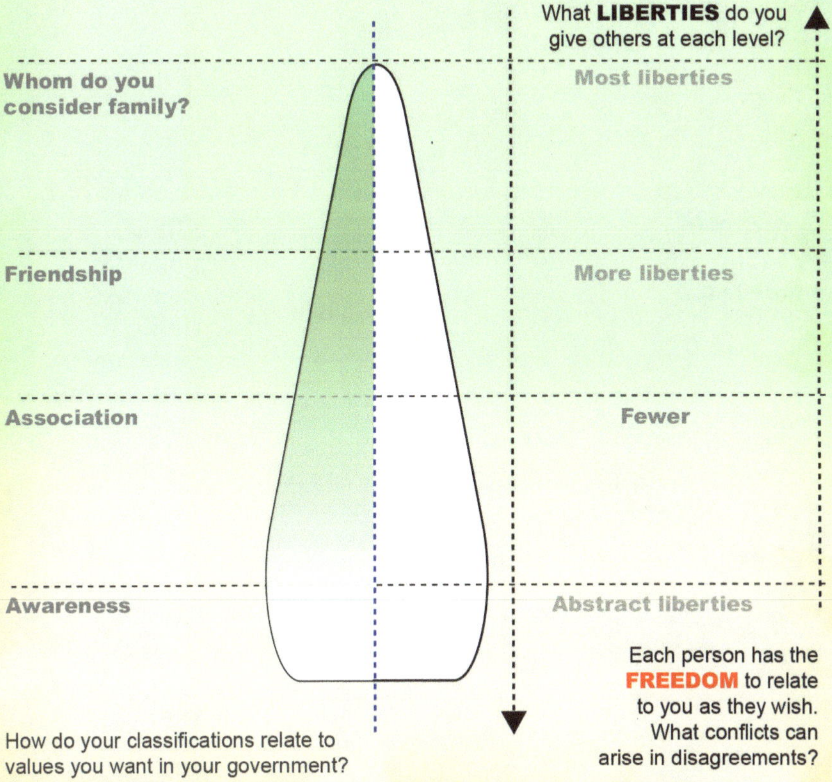

What **LIBERTIES** do you give others at each level?

Whom do you consider family?

Most liberties

Friendship

More liberties

Association

Fewer

Awareness

Abstract liberties

How do your classifications relate to values you want in your government?

Each person has the **FREEDOM** to relate to you as they wish. What conflicts can arise in disagreements?

What then must we do? Leo Tolstoy

FREEDOM EQUALITY

FREEDOM disrupts **EQUALITY**, both constancy of character and distribution.

Time 1

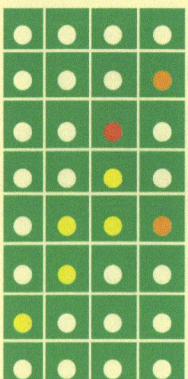

Expectation: variation unpredicted

Time 2

Process modification

Time 3

FREEDOM promotes change, choice, and deviation in time sequences.

EQUALITY suppresses individuality of character and **FREEDOM** of motion.

Time 1

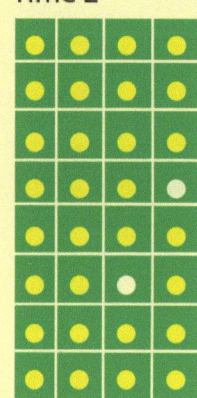

Regulates sequences of experience.

Time 2

Expectation: variation predictable

Time 3

EQUALITY discourages novelty and promotes distribution and security.

Marx Linear Direction of Social/Political History
Excludes a Feedback Loop*

Total **FREEDOM** obscures perception of relationships and creates unpredictable change

Total **EQUALITY** obscures perception of individuality and creates stasis

Tribes   Capitalism   Socialism

**FREEDOM
ONE** Man
NOBLE or SAVAGE?

Clans   Tribes

Complete freedom creates power and energy but leads to survival of the fittest and chaos

Marx/Hegelian Dialectic model is entropic and therefore results in both equality and social stasis.

Communism   World order

EVERY Man
COMRADESHIP or
UNIFORMITY?
EQUALITY

* *Cycle is clockwise and with a feedback loop because it is necessary for the continuation of history, which requires the recognition of change.*

Without reciprocating influences of **FREEDOM** and **EQUALITY** moderating each other, each value in isolation may lead to the following application scenarios:

Isolation of **EQUALITY** requires that any regard for rights of the individual (**FREEDOM**) must be subordinated to the community of men (**EVERY**).Pursuit of **EQUALITY** disregards **NATURAL LAW** and may extend to the **PAST**, **PRESENT**, and **FUTURE** to affirm itself.

Isolation of **FREEDOM** requires that any regard for community (**EVERY**) must be subordinated to the **NATURAL RIGHTS** of the individual. These rights begin with the life of a man and end with his death. Man's natural relationship with other men is elevated above the animal predator-prey relationship when men refrain from actions to other men they do not desire done to themselves.

The operation of Natural Rights alone creates a biological life cycle of which all mankind is a part. As in the rest of nature this cycle sometimes is chaotic and proceeds according to its own devices. In isolation **FREEDOM** promotes that man functions best when he acts in accord with nature. Thus, it is an act of process ecology not to interfere with natural evolution. When disregarded, the disparities of individual abilities, experience and environment have historically led to the most fit of societies gaining domination over the weak.Then distribution disparities of basic food, shelter, clothing, and other services can create social conflict, a **MASTER-SLAVE** relationship, and/or war.

Pursuit of **EQUALITY** can include attempts to modify natural outcomes through modification of past, present and future conditions which are viewed to promote **EQUALITY**. This **"PROGRES-SIVE"** methodology includes regulations or "affirmative action". It may or may not achieve the desired or even positive effects. On the other hand, actions may ameliorate negative effects of pure **FREEDOM**. In addition to creating regulations which enable **EQUALITY,** "affirmative action" attempts to address disparities of the past. Today these disparities are cultural, histori- cal and environmental. Future "affirmative action" may also consider that everyone is not born equally. Genetic science can extend the concept of disparity to genetic "affirmative action" or regulations which predispose men to a less diverse gene pool. Any policies that include reparations for inequality issues regarding genetics are expensive and may require tax burdens. These burdens reinforce desire for regula- tion and control of expense. The prevention of genetic and environmental disparities could lead to required genetic testing, financial evaluation for parenthood, and abortion, which is a loss of natural **FREEDOM**.

Summary Thoughts on the Political Circulatory System

At the moment of our birth our first **FREEDOM** is to perceive the concrete world with sight, hearing, smell, and touch. We reach out with infant hands into the void beyond the womb. We are hunters for our mother's milk and learn leadership when we cry for it. After our eyes perceive the three dimensions we decide levels of importance. Who feeds and holds us, who places us in our crib and causes the pain of loneliness? As a predator and a victim, or prey, we learn to evaluate others in regard to our needs. Thus our first concrete experience is **FREEDOM**. Our first abstract understanding is there are others, first objects and then other people. Therefore, we are led, kicking and screaming, from the concretely felt actualization of **I**, which is **FREEDOM**, to the abstract understanding of **I** in regard to **OTHERS**, which is expressed in **EVERY**, or **EVERYONE**. The constant interplay of **I** with others, expressed in **EVERYONE**, creates the behavior solution of: "Treat others as you would have them treat you, **I**." Each **ONE** person constantly evaluates his **FREEDOM** in regard to each other person, or **EVERY**. This is the **EVERYONE PARADOX**. We cannot be **ONE**, the individual, and **EVERY**, all at the same time. Thus the concept expresses a pure abstract form which exists and is hoped for only in our minds. Our "levels of importance",

ordered by our personal history and understanding of human contact, give a practical solution to **EACH PERSON**. This is necessary because the opposition of **ONE** to **EVERY** never collapses and therefore does not create synthesis. Each person creates his own path between them. Individuals beget families, families beget clans and tribes, tribes beget cultures, cultures beget states and nations, and, finally, there is the abstract of the family of man, or **EVERYONE**. Relationship descends from the intensely personal to a vague abstraction. **EACH PERSON**'s criteria may include proximity, race, sex, age, income, language, cultural affinity, religion, politics, aesthetic issues, or specifically personal skills such as writing. In our complex world a **PROGRESSIVISM** which includes the concept of synthesis can only represent a temporal alignment of the political function of government to the needs of existing culture and its relationship of **ONE** to **EVERY**. This is the wish of the **EVERYONE** Tug of War. It becomes the barometer used to gauge the fitness of government to the culture it governs at a specific time. The *United Nations Universal Declaration of Human Rights* reminds us of our desire to somehow achieve this unreachable synthesis. It is our **HOPE** and our **TRAGEDY**.

EACH PERSON wants FREEDOM.
EVERYONE wants EQUALITY.

The space between ONE
and EVERY is mediated by
JUSTICE.

JUSTICE: Highest, most effective combination and/or relationship between the contrasting values of **FREEDOM** and **EQUALITY** within a given duration of TIME and SPACE.

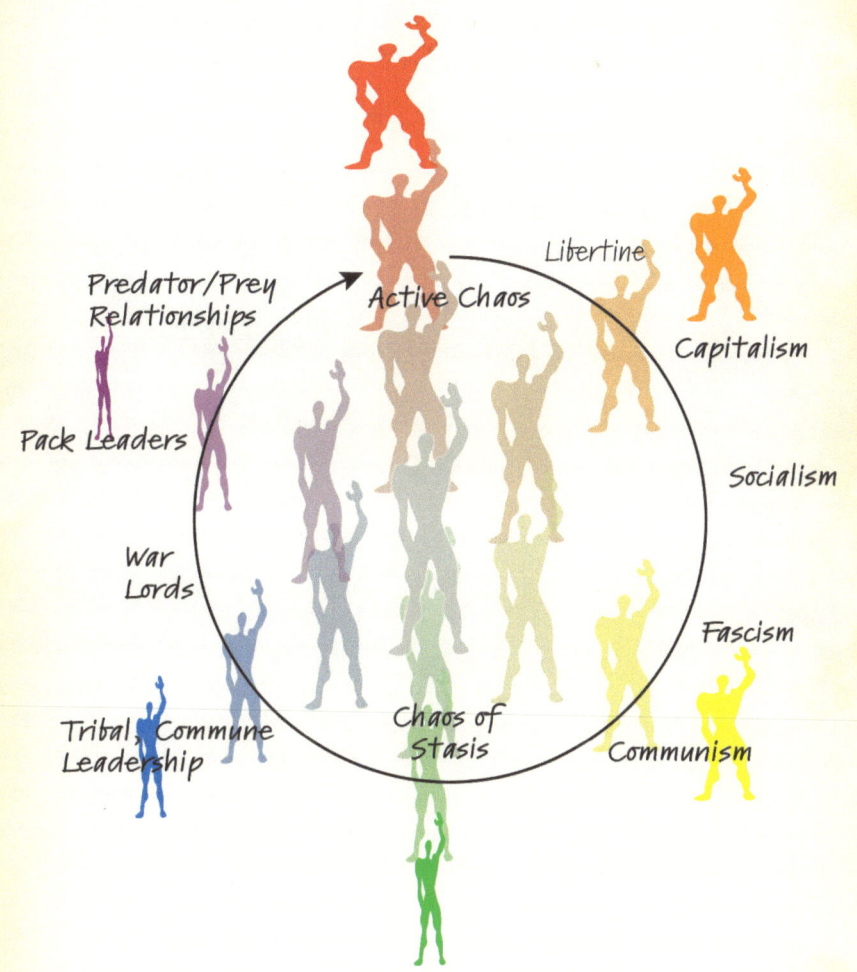

Discrepancies and disassociations of government with the cultural understanding of the **EVERYONE** paradox creates levels of **INJUSTICE.**

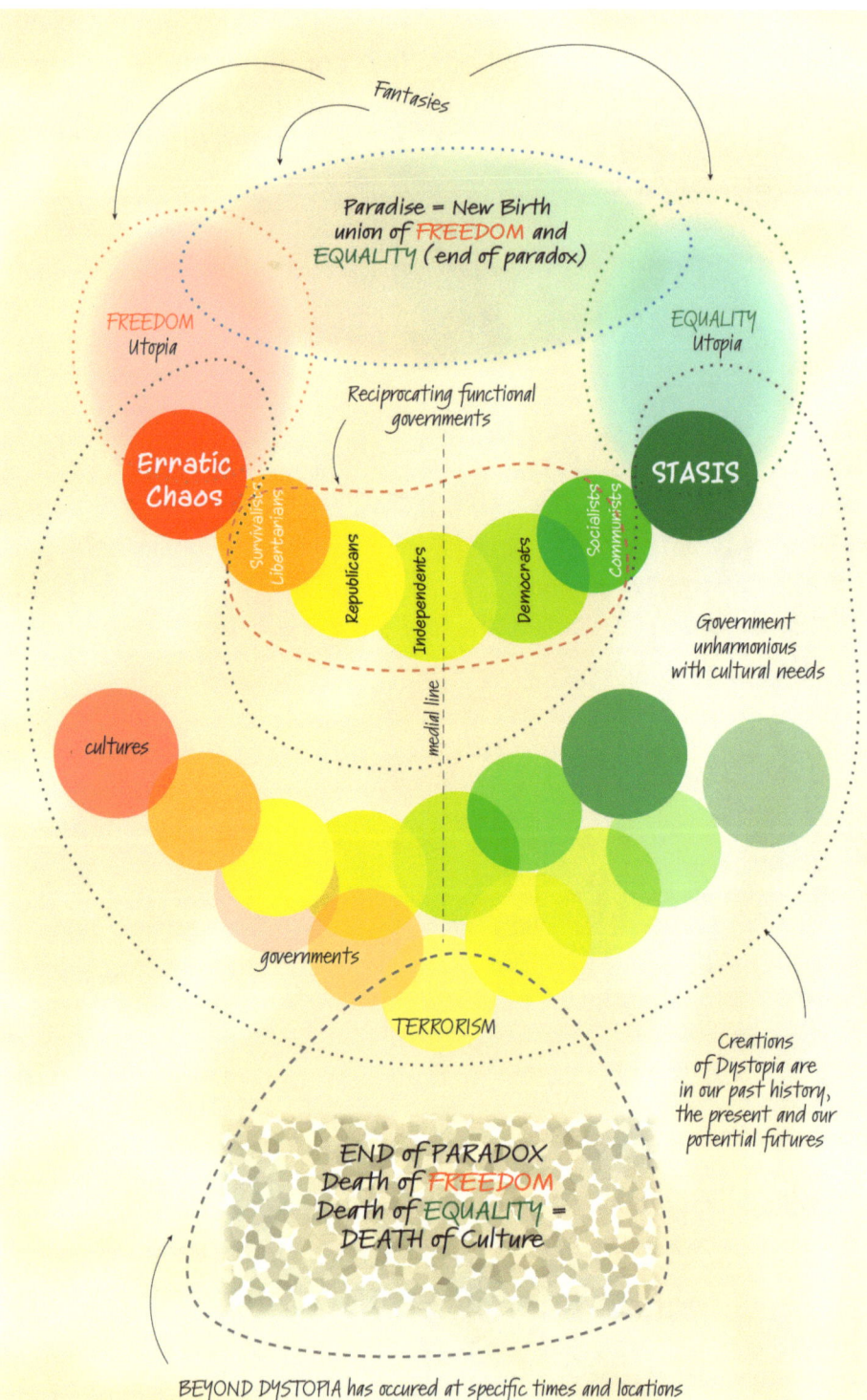

Fantasies

Paradise = New Birth
union of FREEDOM and
EQUALITY (end of paradox)

FREEDOM
Utopia

EQUALITY
Utopia

Reciprocating functional
governments

Erratic
Chaos

STASIS

Survivalists
Libertarians

Republicans

Independents

Democrats

Socialists
Communists

medial line

Government
unharmonious
with cultural needs

cultures

governments

TERRORISM

Creations
of Dystopia are
in our past history,
the present and our
potential futures

END of PARADOX
Death of FREEDOM
Death of EQUALITY =
DEATH of Culture

BEYOND DYSTOPIA has occured at specific times and locations
in man's past and is a potential reality in our future.

Levels of the EVERYONE Paradox

1. Paradise: This fantasy promotes that the progressive advancement of humankind will insure that we percieve an illusion that FREEDOM and EQUALITY are not paradoxical and can wholely occupy the same space.

2. The FREEDOM Utopian obsession and the EQUALITY Utopian obsession will drive cultures to either Erratic Chaos or complete Stasis. It ends in an unrealistic fantasy and potential war and revolution by the opposing utopia.

3. Democracies reciprocating between EQUALITY focused parties and FREEDOM focused parties create a moderate, but balanced, dystopia which subverts the creation of obsessive Utopias.

4. Dystopias are non functional cultures and governments.
   A. Dystopias and wars are created from the creation of Utopias obsessed with either FREEDOM or EQUALITY.
   B. Attempted creation of Paradise fantasies are completely contrary to NATURE.
   C. If a government is not synchronized with its culture's needs and wants chaos will create dystopia.

Literary examples of Dystopias include:
   Brave New World (1932), by Aldous Huxley
   Atlas Shrugged (1957), by Ayn Rand
   A Clockwork Orange (1962), by Anthony Burgess
   The Time Machine (1895), by H.G. Wells

Note: Many dystopian novels provide provide hope through potential escape or revolution.

BALANCING FREEDOM and EQUALITY

CIRCUS OF THE WORLD

Beyond Dystopia is the
STATE of TERROR

...Then they came upon moose. It was a big bull they first found. Here was meat and life, and it was guarded by no mysterious fires nor flying missiles of flame. Splay hoofs and palmated antlers they knew, and they flung their customary patience and caution to the wind. It was a brief fight and fierce. The big bull was beset on every side. He ripped them open or split their skulls with shrewdly driven blows of his great hoofs. He crushed them and broke them on his large horns. He stamped them into the snow under him in the wallowing struggle. But he was foredoomed, and he went down with the she-wolf tearing savagely at his throat, and with other teeth fixed everywhere upon him, devouring him alive, before ever his last struggles ceased or his last damage had been wrought....

White Fang, by Jack London, 1915

In this tale by Jack London the wolves (apex predators) hunt their prey and accomplish the following objectives which are imitated by human predators and terrorists:

1. Prevention of any avenues of escape by the prey
2. Predator must prevent any interference by a third party
3. Destroy any hope of FREEDOM in the prey
4. Acceptance of the superiority of the predator by prey
5. Total submission to the predator's will (end of EQUALITY)
Fear, intellectual and physical exhaustion, and despair result in a state of emptiness (no sense of future). The prey can then be eaten or remodeled according to the desires of human predators.

These objectives have been carried out by families, clans, and nations throughtout history. A few modern examples include concentration camps, the Rape of Nanking, 1978 Jim Jones Massacre of 918 people, ISIS, pirates, and the Democratic Peoples Republic of Korea.

..."THROUGH me you pass into the city of woe:
Through me you pass into eternal pain:
Through me among the people lost for aye.
Justice the founder of my fabric mov'd:
To rear me was the task of power divine,
Supremest wisdom, and primeval love.
Before me things create were none, save things
Eternal, and eternal I endure.

"All hope abandon ye who enter here."

...Here sighs with lamentations and loud moans
Resounded through the air pierc'd by no star,
That e'en I wept at entering. Various tongues,
Horrible languages, outcries of woe,
Accents of anger, voices deep and hoarse,
With hands together smote that swell'd the sounds,
Made up a tumult, that for ever whirls
Round through that air with solid darkness stain'd,
Like to the sand that in the whirlwind flies...

Sellections from Canto III, The Inferno from the Devine Comedy,
by Danre Alighieri, A.D. 1308-1320
translation by Rev. H. F. Cary, M.A., A.D. 1814

All of human energy is revealed in the
Tug of War between
FREEDOM and EQUALITY.
Abandon this TENSION and hope for
EVERYONE is lost.

Communities of location began development when a farmer used a cart to carry his produce to a village. Later, towns, cities, and nations were created. After the invention of railroads and automobiles communities with a mutual interest in survival expanded to the nations we see today. Today's EVERYONE concept is expressed in the idea of the modern geographic nation. Dominating concerns for FREEDOM or EQUALITY may be presented differently from geographic region to region. This may be interpreted as national identity.

Concept of nations or national regions with in common focus on **FREEDOM** or **EQUALITY**

FACEMASKPATHS are the new Silk Roads which create communities of string which net the earth.

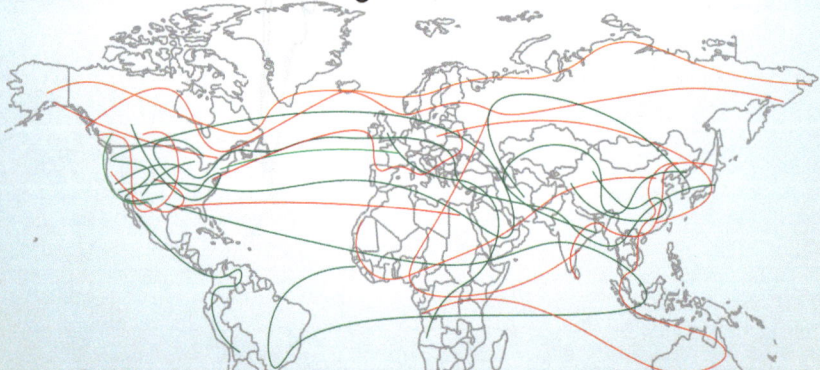

In a world of social media new FACEMASKPATHS create networks of mutual interests, simultaneously transmitted. These are the new Silk Roads of thoughts and feelings. Community of space becomes community of line and net. In common focus of individual people is substituted with identification with electronic images of people, real, masked, or created, which can transform gender, race, nationality or age with electronic will. How will this inpact understanding for individuals and the nation states upon which EVERYONE relies? How will a United Nations deal with this multiplication of causes and effects? What is ONE? Is it a person, or is EVERY mask created in a social cloud a person too? Can we discern the difference? Again, in this electronic world we still live with the same question and PARADOX.

Who is EVERYONE?

POSTFIX

There is a long tradition in art to investigate the world and attempt to organize forms and visualize processes which help us to understand what we perceive with our senses and what we feel about those experiences. Some of these traditions have interwoven with scientific investigation. Examples include Andreas Vesalius' anatomical illustrations, photography by Eadweard Muybridge, Goethe's study of optics, and countless artist draftsmen documenting paleontology and archaeology discoveries. Josef Albers in Interaction of Color, Le Corbusier in Le Modulor, and Ozenfant in Foundations of Modern Art are artists who attempted to ascribe some understandable form to seemingly unrelated experiences. In the last half of the last century science and art created a new codex, built on the interrelation of graphic image, set theory, and language. It combined the pictograph with the phonic alphabet of the English language. The social scientist creates charts and graphs, showing data trends describing the real world. This codex of pictographs and the phonic alphabet has played its part. I see no reason why artists cannot continue to participate in the organization of that understanding using a similar codex, a sort of personal social sketching. This personal sketch is meant to stir the imagination to consider possibilities perhaps not fully charted.

Glen Smith

. . .

38:4 Where wast thou when I laid the foundations of the earth? declare, if thou hast understanding.

38:5 Who hath laid the measures thereof, if thou knowest? or who hath stretched the line upon it?

38:6 Whereupon are the foundations thereof fastened? or who laid the corner stone thereof;

38:7 When the morning stars sang together, and all the sons of God shouted for joy?

38:8 Or who shut up the sea with doors, when it brake forth, as if it had issued out of the womb? . . .

. . .

42:1 Then Job answered the LORD, and said,

42:2 I know that thou canst do every thing, and that no thought can be withholden from thee.

42:3 Who is he that hideth counsel without knowledge? therefore have I uttered that I understood not; things too wonderful for me, which I knew not. . . .

The Book of Job, <u>The King James Bible</u>, A.D. 1611

FREEDOM

EQUALITY

PARADOX